THE JBL S

60 Years of Audio Innovation

THE JBL STORY

60 Years of Audio Innovation

By John M. Eargle

ISBN-13: 978-1-4234-1281-6
ISBN-10: 1-4234-1281-8

Published by:
Hal Leonard Corporation
7777 W. Bluemound Road
P.O. Box 13819
Milwaukee, WI 53213

Library of Congress Cataloging-in-Publication Data

Eargle, John.
    The JBL story : 60 years of audio innovation / by John M. Eargle. -- 1st ed.
        p. cm.
    Includes index.
    ISBN 978-1-4234-1281-6
    1. Sound--Equipment and supplies--History. 2. James B. Lansing Sound--History. 3. Sound--Recording and reproducing--United
States--History. 4. Audio equipment industry--United States--History. I. Title.
    TK7881.4.E165 2007
    338.7'6202--dc22
                    2006038246

Printed in China through Colorcraft Ltd, Hong Kong

First Edition

Visit Hal Leonard Online at
www.halleonard.com

Contents

Foreword

I was honored when my friends at JBL asked me to write a Foreword to their Sixtieth Anniversary Book. I first met Jim Lansing in 1943 when he was putting the finishing touches on his 604 coaxial speaker, which was to become one of the great monitor speakers of all time. That meeting went like this:

I had been invited to Jim's lab on Vine Street in Hollywood, and there was a man talking into a small horn. (Actually, it was the high frequency horn section of the 604.) "How does it sound now?" he asked. "A little muffled," said the technician who was working with him; "it was quite a bit louder when you were standing in the middle of the room." Then, the man asked me what I thought. I said "yes, the midrange is about six decibels lower, but the high end is way down." The man then said, "what's your name?" "Les Paul," I replied. The man then said, "I'm Jim Lansing; let's go out and get a bite." It was the beginning of a long friendship.

Three years later, after we had all come back from the War, I was wondering what directions modern music would take. In 1946, Colonel Richard Ranger showed me one of the first Magnetophone tape recorders from Germany, along with his Rangertone machine, and I immediately envisioned putting an additional head in the tape path for doing sound-on-sound recording. A little later, Bing Crosby, working with Jack Mullin, made plans for using one of the machines for delayed West Coast broadcasting of his radio shows.

Later, when Ampex was manufacturing its version of the machine, it was largely at my insistence that they added Sel-Sync to these machines, enabling engineers and artists to lay down extra tracks, like I was doing. This led directly to the first Ampex 8-track machines during the mid-fifties — and the rest is recording history.

It was also in 1946 that Jim Lansing founded a new company known as JBL. Jim's directions turned toward a new generation of speakers, such as the renowned D130, that were to play a vital part in the development of the amplified guitar and the new music of the day — pop, jazz, or whatever — and also led to the concert sound industry we know today.

It turns out that Jim himself was not just a speaker engineer, but also a great fan of music and musicians. He loved his art, and we considered him to be the only speaker guy we could talk to. He was truly "our man" in technology.

Personally, I have always felt a kinship with JBL. Over the years, we've both worked, each in our own ways, to improve music making. So, JBL, here's to your 60th anniversary — and may your next 60 years be as fruitful! Remember, it's all about the music!

Les Paul
Mahwah, New Jersey, July 2006

Preface

The writing of The JBL Story has taken a little over one year and has been an exciting trip all the way. It begins with a corporate history that draws on interviews with many old-timers who actually knew and worked with Jim Lansing, and then wends its way forward to the present. The highlights of JBL's contribution to loudspeaker technology are covered in graphic and technical detail, as are the many facets of JBL's unique approach to company graphic standards via logos and advertising.

The heart of the book is presented in nine chapters that cover the major product areas JBL has addressed. Here, you will see sixty years of consumer products, starting with the humble "original four" items in Jim Lansing's catalog, moving on through the first era of cost-no-object "statement products," then through a long period of forward looking industrial and technical design, and finally to the most recent round of statement products.

By contrast, JBL's Professional Division is only about thirty-five years old, but it has left its own imprint in many areas. JBL Pro is seen and heard in motion picture theaters, sports facilities, performance venues, and is one of the leading providers of loudspeakers for the highly visible tour sound market. The eight vertical markets of JBL Pro are covered in depth through illustrations of noted installations.

The company was founded at the beginning of the high fidelity era, a distinctly American institution. Those of you who remember those heady post-war years will recall the enthusiasm and sheer fun of it all. Not many of those early companies exist today, largely because they lacked long-term knowledgeable corporate guidance. JBL has had the great fortune of having its destiny shaped by two notable men of HiFi, William Thomas and Sidney Harman. It is to them that this book is dedicated.

John Eargle
November 2006

Acknowledgments

Many persons at JBL Professional and JBL Consumer have directly contributed to this book by providing and reviewing copy, identifying and providing photographs, and by expediting all the foregoing in order to meet deadlines. Mark Gander, Vice President of Marketing for JBL Professional, is chief among the many who deserve my thanks, and next of course are Paul Bente, President of JBL Consumer and John Carpanini, President of JBL Professional.

I also want to thank the following persons at JBL Professional: Vice Presidents Ted Leamy and David Scheirman, Directors Peter Chaikin, Charles Goodsell, Simon Jones, and Rick Kamlet; Regional Directors Jim Bumgardner, Perry Celia, and Jon Pierson for identifying and rounding up photos and collateral data on various installations. Brad Ricks deserves special thanks for his technical input on many of the stadium and arena installations. Thanks also to Kerry Kapin and Aaron Huebner (Mbox Design) for identifying specific photos in JBL's archives and other sources.

The staff of Stereo Sound in Japan is also acknowledged for their sharing of photos and other data, as are Don McRitchie and Steve Schell, masters of the Audioheritage and Lansingheritage websites. Also acknowledged are Doug Daniel for rounding up data from overseas distributors and Chris Neumann for providing data on the Synthesis Product Group.

I also want to thank John Cianti, Erin Cody, and Mike Casa of JBL Consumer for photos, and engineers Doug Button (JBL Pro), and Greg Timbers and Jerry Moro (JBL Consumer) for review of technical copy and line drawings.

Too numerous to mention here are the dealers, distributors, photographers, system designers, and consultants who played important roles in many of the installations shown in this book. Their contributions are acknowledged in the copy accompanying each installation panel.

Last and far from least, we would all like to thank the amazing Les Paul for his support of JBL over many years, as well as the great foreword he wrote to honor this book.

Chapter 1: A Corporate History of JBL:
Introduction and Early Years

Of all American loudspeaker companies, JBL holds the record for overall longevity and product renown. Worldwide, you will hear JBL loudspeakers in more than half of all motion picture theaters and high-level music reinforcement events. It is a good bet that any recording you hear will have been monitored or mastered over JBL loudspeakers at some stage in its production. JBL is heard in the home in music systems, in surround sound systems for video, in a variety of computer systems, and in the highest quality factory-equipped automobile sound systems.

The company we know today as JBL Incorporated dates from 1946 and had its roots in earlier companies founded by James Bullough Lansing. Relatively little is known of the early years of Lansing, and we are thankful for the personal recollections of several family members—including brother Bill Martin, Lansing's widow Glenna, and daughter Lois O'Neil—given at various times during the last 25 years. Further reminiscences of Lansing's early business career were provided by Alvis Ward, former President of Altec Lansing, early technical colleagues John Blackburn and John Hilliard, and business associates William Thomas, John Edwards, and Bart Locanthi during the early years of James B. Lansing Sound, Incorporated. The legendary guitarist Les Paul has also contributed reminiscences of his meetings with Lansing during the late 1940s.

Jim Lansing was born James Martini, 14 January 1902, in Macoupin County, Illinois, and was the ninth of thirteen children of Henry Martini, and Grace Erbs. Both parents hailed from the Midwest. Henry Martini was involved in coal mining with responsibilities that took the family to several locations in the Midwest. In his later teens, Jim lived briefly with a Bullough family in Litchfield, IL, and he eventually took their name when he changed his surname to Lansing.

Like many boys in their early teens, he was fascinated by anything electrical or mechanical. His interest in Leyden jars and crystal radios ultimately resulted in his building a small radio transmitter that apparently caused enough local interference to warrant an order to shut it down.

Lansing attended Lawrence Middle School and high school in nearby Springfield. In his late teens he attended a business college and worked for a time as an auto mechanic, specializing in precision repair work. Spare auto parts were often hard to come by, and Lansing developed the necessary skills in the machine shop to make many of these parts himself.

Lansing's mother died in 1924, and at that time he decided to move on. After a short sea-going stint as a radio telegrapher, he settled in Salt Lake City. His future bride, Glenna Peterson, tells of meeting Lansing there in 1925 while he was working for a local radio station. At about this same time he met his future business partner, Kenneth G. Decker. Lansing had in the meantime been bitten by the loudspeaker bug and was intent on manufacturing them. (No detail of loudspeaker building would have seemed difficult for one skilled in automotive machining.)

Lansing and Decker had actually set up a small manufacturing operation in Salt Lake City, but they soon decided that there would be greater opportunities in Los Angeles, a major center at the time for radio set manufacturing.

James B. Lansing
(1902–1949), circa 1925.
Photo courtesy Lois O'Neil

Lansing Manufacturing Company

Lansing and Decker moved to Los Angeles in 1927 and established the Lansing Manufacturing Company (LMC), whose major products were 6- and 8-inch cone loudspeakers intended primarily for radio sets and consoles. Before organizing the new company, Jim had legally changed his name to James Bullough Lansing, and a new birth certificate was eventually issued in that name in 1942. (Most of his brothers had previously changed their surnames to Martin.)

Younger brother Bill Martin moved to California to join Lansing's new venture, and another brother, George, made the trek west later. Initially, the company operated as a cottage industry, with family members making seamed paper cones and winding voice coils in the evenings at home for assembly into finished loudspeakers at the factory the next day. The company's first location was on Santa Barbara Boulevard. After an interim location at 6626 McKinley Avenue, the company established its permanent headquarters in 1934 at 6900 McKinley Avenue in South Los Angeles.

In the late 1920s the success of *Don Juan* and *The Jazz Singer* inaugurated the sound era for motion pictures. With no manufacturing capabilities allied with the motion picture industry itself, Western Electric, the manufacturing arm of American Telephone and Telegraph (AT&T), soon filled the void and became the dominant force in making equipment for the fledgling industry.

Kenneth G. Decker
(1896–1939), circa 1920.

The vast technical resources of Bell Telephone Laboratories offered many solutions to problems in recording, reproducing, and the allied arts, and they were able to mobilize that technology for manufacturing in a fairly short time.

Earliest LMC product in JBL archives, an 8-inch electro-dynamic model employing a field coil for magnetizing.

Electrical Research Products Incorporated (ERPI) was organized as a manufacturing and distributing company by Western Electric (WE), specifically for servicing the motion picture industry at both the studio and exhibition levels.

The early WE theater loudspeakers were basically one-way designs, consisting of a large curved "snail shell" exponential horn whose frequency response was band-limited to the range from about 100 Hz to 5000 Hz. In time, Western Electric added a high-frequency unit as well as a set of low-frequency 18-inch drivers to augment the response of these systems.

Western Electric 5A horn with 555 driver, which covered the range from about 100 Hz to 5000 Hz

Earliest known LMC advertisement, dating from 1928, for a loudspeaker enclosure with integral driver.

Western Electric three-way
system, introduced in 1931.

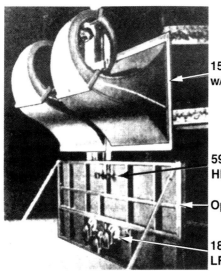

15A horns
w/555 drivers

596 Bostwick
HF units

Open baffle

18-inch
LF units

Eighteen-inch woofers in a large open-back baffle, along with a high frequency horn-driver unit, extended the response of the basic system downward to about 50 Hz and upward to about 8 kHz.

The Hollywood technical community was not satisfied with either of these designs put forth by WE, and the sound department at Metro-Goldwyn-Mayer (MGM) Studios took special disagreement with the augmented three-way WE system. Specifically, they objected to the 12-foot path length of the midrange portion, with its high signal transit delay time, relative to the low- and high-frequency sections. They were equally dissatisfied with the standard RCA cinema system of that time, which consisted of a single 8-inch cone mounted on a straight low-frequency horn.

In 1933, a frustrated Douglas Shearer, brother of movie star Norma Shearer and head of the MGM sound department, came to the conclusion that he could build a better system than either WE or RCA. With the help of a young electrical engineer named John Hilliard he assembled a team of experts that included Robert Stephens (later of Stephens TruSonic) and physicist John Blackburn, a graduate of California Institute of Technology. Among them, they identified LMC as the most likely source for both electrical and loudspeaker components. Obviously Decker's marketing acumen and Lansing's mechanical and manufacturing skills were about to pay off.

Over the next two years the so-called Shearer-Lansing system was defined and perfected. It was a large two-way system consisting of a high frequency multicellular horn (manufactured by the MGM set department) and a W-shaped low-frequency horn enclosure. The smaller model 500-A was used in screening rooms, dubbing theaters, and early sound reinforcement.

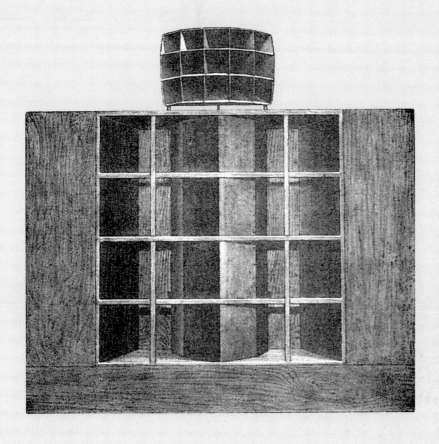

Shearer-Lansing two-way system, which covered the range from 40 Hz to 10 kHz.

The smaller model 500-A, was used in screening rooms, dubbing theaters, and early sound reinforcement.

The machine shop at
6900 McKinley Avenue.
The circular pieces are outer
cases for high-frequency drivers.

When the Shearer system was introduced, WE objected to Lansing's use of an annular-slit model high-frequency driver, inasmuch as they had already been issued a patent on that basic design.

As a counter to this, Blackburn and Lansing designed a radial-slit high-frequency driver, the model 285, as an interim step in the evolution of the Shearer system. While reviewing the patent literature, Blackburn later discovered prior art for the annular-slit design dating from developments in the acoustical phonograph from the early years of the 20th century, so LMC was now free to reintroduce the traditional annular-slit phasing plug in the high-frequency driver.

In addition to the large theater version of the system, a smaller model was designed for mid-size theaters and screening facilities. For extremely large houses, a "Y-throat" adapter was designed to accommodate a pair of compression drivers.

During the late 1930s Lansing developed the Iconic system, a small two-way system using a 15-inch low-frequency driver in a small, vented, direct radiator enclosure and a small-format high-frequency compression driver that fed a small multicellular horn. The Iconic system attained wide popularity throughout the motion picture industry as a monitor, and the basic system configuration, with only minor improvements, is still the basis for many of today's studio monitor designs. It was also offered as a high-end system for home use with a furniture finish and a decorative grille.

The great success of the Shearer-MGM connection helped LMC in other product fields. The company continued to provide products for the film industry as well as for a variety of early professional sound reinforcement applications. The company's success depended on the synergy of its principals, so when Ken Decker was killed in Army Air Corps maneuvers in 1939, the fortunes of LMC took a downward turn.

A watershed event in the history of professional sound had taken place in 1938 when the United States Government decided to undo the virtual monopoly that WE held in the field of motion picture sound.

The Lansing Iconic system.
Utility model (A); consumer
model (B). JBL archives

The 6900 McKinley Avenue plant, circa 1942, after purchase by Altec Service Corporation. JBL archives

WE was forced to divest itself of certain holdings in the sound reproducing field, including loudspeakers and amplifiers. WE signed a consent decree, and all of their pertinent manufactured inventory holdings were sold for a nominal sum to a group of engineers who worked for them at the time. These engineers formed a new company, Altec Service Corporation, independent of Western Electric. (The name Altec is a contraction of "all technical," signifying the new company's mission.) The principals of the new company were George Carrington and E. L. Conrow.

Altec Service Corporation maintained service contracts with motion picture chains across the country and went about their business as before. After about two years the company was running low on its basic stock of replacement parts that had been inherited from the spin-off, and it became apparent to Carrington and Conrow that the company would have to develop a source for new manufactured items if they were to remain a viable force in the service business.

By 1941 LMC was in dire straights, and it had become apparent to Lansing that the sale of LMC was the only way to keep the company afloat. Carrington and Conrow were very aware of Lansing's predicament and approached him regarding a merger of Altec Service Corporation and LMC. According to Alvis Ward, a former President of Altec Lansing, Altec Service Corporation purchased the nearly destitute LMC in December of 1941 for $50,000, and the company was renamed Altec Lansing Corporation (ALC). At the time there were 19 employees in the LMC organization; Lansing signed a 5-year contract with the new company and assumed the position of Vice President of Engineering.

WE agreed to license to ALC rights to manufacture royalty-free any and all of the proprietary designs that were covered by the consent decree. Thus, ALC inherited all product rights from both WE and LMC, clearly placing under one umbrella the broadest catalog, and certainly the best products, in the field of professional sound.

A Reprinted from the Journal of the Society of Motion Picture Engineers, Vol. 45, No. 5 (November, 1945), Pp. 339–349

AN IMPROVED LOUDSPEAKER SYSTEM FOR THEATERS*

J. B. LANSING AND J. K. HILLIARD**

Summary.—*This paper gives a description of a new 2-way loudspeaker for theaters. New permanent magnet low-frequency and high-frequency units having replaceable diaphragms are described. These units are combined in a horn system having the following advantages: A higher efficiency, extended frequency range, permanent magnet units providing higher air gap flux densities, elimination of backstage radiation from the diaphragms, better transient response, and an improved over-all presence.*

B

Altec Lansing A-4 Voice of the Theatre® system. Header from SMPTE Journal, May 1945 (A); photo of system (B).

Altec Lansing Corporation

John K. Hilliard (1902–1989),
circa 1942. JBL archives

With the stability offered by the merger, Lansing was at last free to pursue his work without financial worry.

This was the positive side of the new relationship; the negative side was that he was no longer in charge and now had to function as a staff member taking orders from others. During the war years, ALC assumed a number of military contracts, including development work on an airborne submarine detection system that made use of advanced magnet materials. Lansing himself was kept busy, however, in loudspeaker development. During his five-year tenure at ALC, he perfected many of the processes that have since become standard in loudspeaker manufacturing around the world—specifically, high-speed winding of ribbon wire voice coils on metal mandrels, and the hydraulic forming of high-frequency aluminum diaphragms.

Meanwhile, John Hilliard, a former colleague in the Shearer-MGM project, had joined ALC in a management capacity. John had a knack for getting things done within a corporate environment, and the collaboration of both Lansing and Hilliard ensured that several important projects were carried through. The primary effort here was the development of the Voice of the Theatre® series of cinema systems, for which both men took design credit.

The model A-4 inaugurated the Voice of the Theatre® series, which kept Altec Lansing at the forefront of the motion picture exhibition industry over a 40-year span until the mid-1980s. Similar in overall size to the earlier Shearer-Lansing system, it had a large ported low-frequency section with its dual woofers additionally front-loaded with a straight horn. The multicellular high-frequency section was driven with the 288 driver, a 3-inch diaphragm design with an aluminum ribbon wire voice coil. The low-frequency drivers were the model 515, a 15-inch diameter design with a 3-inch aluminum voice coil and the first 15-inch low-frequency driver to make use of flat wire. The Voice of the Theatre® systems also made use of new magnet materials, obviating the traditional requirement for field coil power supplies.

Another significant product for which Lansing could take all design credits was the world-renowned model 604 Duplex® loudspeaker. According to ALC, radio broadcaster Art Crawford had suggested that the company design a two-way coaxial monitor loudspeaker embodying their leading-edge technology. What eventually emerged as the model 604 combined a small multicellular horn mounted concentrically on a 15-inch woofer, with an 801 high-frequency driver mounted behind and firing along the axis of the system. Introduced in 1944, it soon gained a leading reputation as a broadcast monitor and became one of the most successful monitors in recording history.

When Lansing had sold his company to Altec Service in 1941, it was with the understanding that all previous company trade names, goodwill, and assets would remain the property of the new company. He also agreed that he would not go into competition with ALC for a period of five years. While there were continuing disagreements with Carrington during this period, Lansing honored the contract to the letter until its expiration in 1946. Lansing was then free to enter the loudspeaker business on his own, and it came as a surprise to no one at Altec Lansing when he announced his intentions to do so. Generally, the parting was amicable—but no one at Altec Lansing was prepared for the success that would ultimately accrue to Lansing's new venture.

A

THE DUPLEX LOUDSPEAKER*

JAMES B. LANSING**

Summary.—*The Duplex Loudspeaker is a combined two-way loudspeaker mounted in an integral unit so that the high-frequency energy is radiated from a small multicellular horn mounted on the face of the low-frequency diaphragm.*

Separate permanent magnets of improved magnetic material are now used for the fields of each voice coil.

The crossover has been selected at 1200 cycles so that the high-frequency horn can be placed in the center of the low-frequency diaphragm.

A signal input up to 25 w can safely be applied to the speaker. The intermodulation products are very low as a result of the two-way principle. The configuration of the high-frequency horn produces an angle of radiation which is 60 degrees in the horizontal plane and 40 degrees in the vertical plane. Due to the type of construction a high degree of uniformity between units can be maintained in manufacture.

The unit is capable of efficient radiation beyond 15,000 cycles.

B

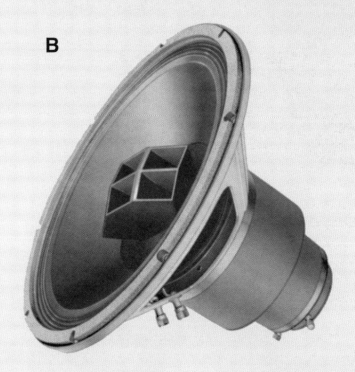

Altec Lansing 604 Duplex® loudspeaker system. Header from 1945 SMPTE Journal paper (A) photo of loudspeaker (B).

LANSING SOUND, INC.

MODEL D 101
GENERAL PURPOSE LOUD SPEAKER

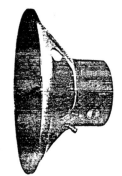

A 15 inch general purpose loud speaker with exceptionally high efficiency and wide dynamic range. It is especially suited for Public Address and music system use.

The cone frame is of cast aluminum for high rigidity and light weight. An Aluminum diaphragm fastened directly to the 3 inch voice coil tube extends the high frequency range.

The Heavy Alnico V magnet is entirely enclosed in a heavy field case to hold stray magnetic fields to a minimum. It can be used near Cathode ray or television tubes without effecting their performance.

SPECIFICATIONS

- Power Input—20 Watts
- Impedance—15 Oms
- Resonant Frequency—55 Cycles
- Outside Diameter—15-3 16"
- Depth—7¾"
- Field—Permanent Magnet
- Voice Coil—3" Diameter Wound with Aluminum Ribbon
- Mounting Dimensions—R. M. A. Standard
- Net Weight—29 Lbs.
- Shipping Weight—33 Lbs.

The company that is presently known as JBL, Incorporated, was first called Lansing Sound, Incorporated, and dated from 1 October 1946. The principals of the company were James B. Lansing, Chauncy Snow, and financial consultant Chester L. Noble. Since the designation Lansing had been identified for so many years as a product trade name, it was only logical that ALC should take immediate issue with the name of the new company. By out-of-court agreement with Carrington, Lansing Sound, Incorporated, changed its name to James B. Lansing Sound, Incorporated, a change that satisfied all concerned, inasmuch as it drew attention to the man himself rather than to specific products.

The earliest letterhead of the new company gave the corporate address as 510 South Spring Street in Los Angeles, which was the office of Chester Noble. The letterhead also referred to a factory location in San Marcos, a small town fairly close to Oceanside in San Diego County on ranch property that Lansing owned. Lansing maintained a complete machine shop on the premises, and it was here where he actually began his new loudspeaker manufacturing efforts.

The first product introduced by James B. Lansing Sound, Incorporated, was the model D 101 15-inch loudspeaker, a near-copy of the earlier Altec Lansing model 515 with the addition of an aluminum dome and back air venting through the voice coil former. Also, with some recklessness, Lansing used the Iconic emblem on this model. Right out of the gate, Lansing was flying in the face of his previous employers, and he was further asked to cease and desist in the use of the trademarked Iconic name.

Lansing soon developed a series of components that enabled him to put together a virtual copy of the original Iconic loudspeaker system, including the model D 101 15-inch woofer, a high-frequency driver of the Altec Lansing 802 class, and a small multicellular horn. The high-frequency driver, known as the model D175, remained in the JBL catalog through the 1970s.

Specification sheet for Lansing Sound model D 101.

Lansing pioneered the use of 4-inch ribbon wire voice coils for low-frequency drivers. The D130 was the first 15-inch model to incorporate this. When the D130 was introduced in 1947, the D 101 was discontinued. The development of Alnico V during the war years made the new 4-inch voice coil designs possible. Working with Robert Arnold of Arnold Engineering Company in Chicago, Lansing was able to procure a magnet of reasonable size that could saturate a 4-inch diameter voice coil gap with a magnetic field strength of about 12,000 gauss. Such a gap obviously had to be quite narrow, and the relatively large voice coil had to be manufactured with a degree of precision heretofore unknown in the loudspeaker industry. Other products designed by Lansing during this same period included the 12-inch D131 and 8-inch D208 and D216 cone drivers.

James B. Lansing at Fletcher Drive plant in 1948–49. JBL archives

The company had been formed during the economic slump immediately following World War II. As we have noted earlier, Lansing was rarely focused on business affairs, and financial problems surfaced almost immediately. In November of 1947 Lansing secured additional funding from aviation pioneer Roy Marquardt. With this agreement, Marquardt Aviation Company agreed to provide manufacturing space for a cost to Lansing of 10 percent of net sales, with the Marquardt corporation retaining the right to take assignment of accounts receivable to satisfy at any time the amount due. Marquardt further agreed to lend money to Lansing for working capital in such amounts as would not be a burden on the Marquardt corporation itself. The Marquardt corporation was further given an option on 40 percent of the stock of the Lansing company.

The Marquardt corporation was represented on Lansing's Board of Directors by its treasurer, William H. Thomas. With the new financial arrangements in place, Lansing moved his offices and manufacturing facilities to the Marquardt plant located at 4221 Lincoln Boulevard in Venice, California. In late 1948, the company moved into the Marquardt facility at 7801 Hayvenhurst Avenue in Van Nuys, California.

At the end of its second fiscal year in 1948, James B. Lansing Sound, Incorporated, showed an operating loss of $2500—and this with most of the tooling investment costs still in the process of being capitalized. By December of 1948 Lansing's debt to Marquardt had reached almost $14,000, and it was inevitable that the company would have to be taken over by Marquardt, with Lansing remaining on the payroll as an employee. At that time Lansing bought up the company interests held by Messrs. Snow and Noble so that he became sole spokesman for his company.

William H. Thomas (1912–1995), circa 1948. JBL archives

In early 1949 Marquardt was purchased by General Tire Company, who was not interested in maintaining the relationship with Lansing, and the tie was thus severed. William Thomas, having developed a flair for the loudspeaker business, chose to leave Marquardt and became a vice president in the Lansing company. James B. Lansing, Incorporated, vacated the Marquardt facility and moved to its fourth location in three years, 2439 Fletcher Drive, Los Angeles. During Lansing's final three years he had developed a close business relationship with Robert Arnold of Arnold Engineering, the primary supplier of Alnico V material for the domestic loudspeaker industry.

At various points in this relationship, Lansing accrued large debts to Arnold—but somehow Arnold always extended his most generous terms to the company. In reading the Lansing correspondence file with Arnold Engineering, it is clear that there was high mutual respect between these two men. It was also apparent that Arnold considered Lansing the most influential manufacturer in an industry that was slow to adopt new methods and materials. He may have seen in Lansing the image of leadership required to convince the rest of the industry to make the move to Alnico V.

As we read through the Arnold correspondence we can see the physical and emotional toll that hard times had on Lansing. The constant moving of the company was not without its adverse effects on production, and there were never enough funds to pay all suppliers. Perhaps Lansing's growing depression came from the realization that history was about to repeat itself. He may finally have been struck by the similarity of events with those of eight years earlier. By late 1949 the company had amassed a debt of $20,000, and there were no signs of improvement in the business climate.

Lansing usually stopped by Bill Martin's house on his weekend drive home to San Marcos. While George Martin had joined Lansing's latest venture, Bill had chosen to remain at Altec Lansing, and these weekly visits were a way of keeping in touch. On Thursday, 24 September 1949, Lansing stopped by for the last time. He drove to San Marcos and, despondent over the course of business, took his own life later that evening. He is buried at Inglewood Park Cemetery in South Los Angeles.

Note to John Edwards, company controller, from Lansing regarding much-needed parts for D130 production. JBL archives

A few years earlier Lansing had been wise enough to take out a life insurance policy in the name of the company. The policy was for $10,000, and it was the payment on this policy that enabled Bill Thomas to secure the future of the company.

Lansing had left his one-third share of the company to his wife. During the early fifties Thomas negotiated the purchase of the remaining stock from Glenna Lansing and thus became sole owner of the company.

Fletcher Drive plant, circa 1955. JBL archives

JBL from 1949 to 1969:
The William Thomas Years

During the late 1940s and early 1950s the value of the name Lansing as a trademark was rising rapidly. Although it strictly belonged to ALC, the new company made good use of the name in the style of Jim Lansing "Signature" loudspeakers. The use of the term Signature implied that one could not take a man's name away from him, even though that name had been given or sold previously as a commodity in a business transaction.

A perusal of JBL catalogs of the late forties and early fifties points out that the company's list of products consisted of only four significant loudspeaker drivers, a small 2-by-4 multicellular horn, and a single 1200-Hz dividing network. Thomas knew full well that this situation would have to be rectified if the company was to grow. Since the company was ill-equipped at the time to undertake independent engineering development, Thomas sought cooperative ventures with other parties.

By 1953, the motion picture industry was moving toward stereophonic sound reproduction, using three screen channels and a single surround channel. The new medium for this was a 35-mm film print with four magnetic tracks adjacent to the sprocket holes. The Ampex Corporation and Westrex, the export wing of Western Electric, were heavily invested in magnetic recording, and both had the desire to capitalize on the massive retrofitting of theaters worldwide. The Altec Lansing Corporation was, by virtue of its unique position in the motion picture industry, already poised for leadership in that market and proceeded on its own natural course.

Both Ampex and Westrex approached Thomas and JBL as a possible source of loudspeaker components. Collectively, they agreed that JBL would re-engineer the legendary WE 594 4-inch diaphragm high-frequency compression driver, using Alnico V, and that the driver would become an essential element in both Ampex and Westrex theater loudspeaker systems. JBL, however, would retain all rights to the design. The development was carried out under the direction of noted consulting engineer Bart Locanthi, and costs were shared by the three parties involved. JBL soon found itself with a new catalog item, the model 375, which was the only 4-inch high-frequency compression driver available to the worldwide industry at that time. Quite a coup for a young upstart company!

Hartsfield

Paragon

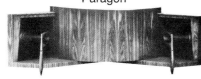

JBL prestige models. Hartsfield, 1954; Paragon, 1957.

075

375

Photo of 075 and cutaway view of 375.

Based on original Bell Laboratories research, Locanthi engineered large-format horn-lens combinations for Westrex and co-engineered a family of large-format radial horns for Ampex. Ampex and Westrex were ultimately unsuccessful in their attempts to enter the motion picture exhibition market, and all of the co-engineered designs became the property of JBL. The former Ampex horns in particular were very successfully integrated into the future JBL Professional line as the 2350-Series.

In 1954 JBL's first flagship product was introduced. The Hartsfield was an elegant corner horn incorporating a new low-frequency driver (model 150-4) and a folded plate acoustic lens driven by the 375 compression driver. The Hartsfield received worldwide accolades, including a rave notice in *LIFE* magazine in 1955 that referred to it as the "ultimate dream loudspeaker."

During these years the services of Alvin Lustig, an unusually talented industrial and graphic designer, were employed. Many of the consumer system enclosures, and much of the sales literature, were produced by him. Later, graphics designer Roger Kennedy joined the fold as JBL's reputation as a leader in high-fidelity products expanded.

At about the same time, JBL began development of the 075 ultra-high-frequency ring radiator. Thomas had long wanted such a device because of its appeal to the burgeoning high-end high-fidelity marketplace. It was introduced in 1957 and immediately was incorporated in many of the larger systems.

With the introduction of the stereophonic LP disc in 1957, Thomas saw an opportunity for the company's next flagship product, the Paragon. The Paragon was a large all-horn system about eight feet wide incorporating a central cylindrical section that acted as a reflector for the cross-firing left and right midrange horns. The basic geometry of the system had been worked out and patented by Richard Ranger for producing a continuous left-to-right set of stereo phantom images in motion picture applications. Noted Berkeley industrial designer Arnold Wolf was responsible for the stunning visual design of the Paragon. Though it clearly speaks to its own era, the design is essentially timeless. More than 1000 Paragons were built by JBL over a 25-year period.

By 1955 JBL could easily boast of having the most complete catalog of high-efficiency loudspeaker hardware available anywhere. The company had cone drivers with 4-inch voice coils, high-frequency drivers with 1.75 and 4-inch diaphragms, and, to top it all off, a "super tweeter" that no one could match.

In less than a decade, JBL had become an unquestioned leader in the high-end high-fidelity market with 1955 sales estimated at about one million dollars.

Up to about 1955 James B. Lansing Sound sold loudspeakers with the Lansing signature logo emblazoned boldly on the magnetic structures. JBL had grown rapidly, and by the mid-1950s it was apparent that the company was becoming a significant force in the marketplace.

View of Casitas Avenue plant, circa 1957. JBL archives

Perforated plate lenses. Large format (Westrex type), upper left; consumer small format, lower right.

Benny Goodman considering the virtues of the Paragon. JBL archives

At ALC, Carrington was pressed by many of his field personnel to do something about this presumed unauthorized use of the Lansing name. Carrington and Alvis Ward of ALC entered into polite out-of-court negotiations with Bill Thomas, and all agreed that the new company would cease and desist from labeling its product as "Lansing."

A brilliant decision was then made by Thomas to label all products as JBL, while retaining the company's name, James B. Lansing Sound, Incorporated. The JBL initials, along with Jerome Gould's new "exclamation point" logo, soon became known worldwide. In a sense, the new logo signified the rapid ascent of the company's fortunes and reputation during the decade from 1955 to 1965.

By 1957 JBL had outgrown the Fletcher Drive facility and made the move to 3249 Casitas Avenue, a location only a few blocks removed from Fletcher Drive. Keeping pace with this growth, a new furniture factory was subsequently built. The company occupied the Casitas premises until 1977 when the move to the current Northridge location was completed.

As we have seen, Bill Thomas had made a strong commitment to design excellence and engineering integrity early on. The next challenge was to cultivate for JBL a larger market share through innovative advertising, alliances with well-known celebrities and artists, and through increased international marketing. Extending over a number of years were a group of JBL corporate image advertisements that appeared in *High Fidelity* and *Audio* magazines. These ads did not address specific products; rather, they emphasized corporate virtues such as manufacturing precision, musicality, and the notion of product development as high art.

As the 1960s got underway it became apparent that large, expensive "furniture-type" high-fidelity systems were giving way to smaller- and mid-sized systems that could deliver substantial low-frequency power. The legacy Lansing low-frequency drivers performed best in large enclosures, and their high efficiency was an asset in the earlier days when few amplifiers could deliver more than about 30 watts. The availability of higher power amplifiers and the requirement for less space pointed to a new direction in cone loudspeaker design.

Bart Locanthi had been joined by noted engineer Edmund May in 1956, and between them they designed a group of new products, the LE-Series of drivers. LE stood for linear efficiency, and this conveyed the design principles of moderate efficiency, extended low-frequency bandwidth, and high linearity at high playback levels. The new drivers gave systems engineers the flexibility of designing smaller floor-standing and bookshelf models that could produce uniform response down to the 35-Hz range at realistic playback levels. By 1963 there were six new drivers in diameters from 15-inches to 2.5 inches, and a new round of systems design was underway with Ed May taking the lead.

Eventually, Thomas began to ponder the future of high-efficiency componentry for high-fidelity purposes. From its inception JBL had based its success on "big" systems for affluent consumers. This domestic market was now showing signs of falling off—while it remained an important one for Japan and the Orient. Thomas's next challenge was to find new domestic and international markets for the company's core high-efficiency products. Thomas had earlier set up a new company, Transducers, Incorporated, specifically for marketing various JBL transducers, primarily to technical users, under a non-JBL logo. Over this period JBL provided a special version of the ring radiator for General Railway Signal for use in rail and automobile traffic monitoring, and a variant of the 375 compression driver for Tideland Signal Corporation, which was used as a fog horn driver for oil platforms and signal buoys in the Gulf of Mexico.

In the early 1950s Leo Fender adopted the D130 as the driver of choice in his high-end guitar amplifier-loudspeaker systems, and a special variation was designed for his company. Musical styles were changing, and the fledgling concert sound industry was about to burst on the scene. Many of these companies identified the advantages of JBL's 4-inch voice coils over the 3-inch models available from other sources, and it was logical to expect that market to flourish. Harvey Gerst, a JBL engineering technician and musician, was involved in product development in this area and provided valuable liaison with many of the third-party companies. In the mid-1960s the "F-Series" was developed to specifically address the musicians' market.

As the sixties progressed, many guitar amplifier manufacturers—including Fender, Sunn, Kustom, and Ampeg—routinely used JBL drivers. This was a clear example of how JBL could carve out for itself a part of the new pro market. Thus began a long dialog between musicians and JBL engineering that continues today.

unquestioned masterpieces of precision

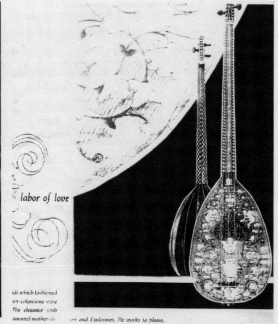

labor of love

ds which fashioned
ity colascione were
The elegance with
inlayed mother-of-
rs and Enclosures, He works to please.

**Art as the
dimension of
imagination.** Unlimited freedom of form; blendings of
color and shapes bending, flowing,
entwining, melting into one another as

**Art as a
component of
perception.** Solid objects broken down into component
elements of light, shade, and texture,
combining to create an undistorted mosaic of
reality; fleeting visual impressions captured

Fanciful ads. Upper left: pyramids for precision; upper right: music for accuracy. Miro (lower left) and
Renoir (lower right) for art in the general sense. Lithographs from William H. Thomas personal collection

There was no Pro Division as such at JBL, but the company made significant progress in this area nonetheless. In 1962 JBL was asked by Capitol Records in Hollywood to develop a new studio monitoring system. The C50SMS7 system, using the new LE-series 15-inch driver and a slant-plate horn-lens combination, was developed by Bart Locanthi in cooperation with Capitol engineers. Through Capitol's connection to EMI Recording in England, the system was soon adopted worldwide by affiliated EMI record companies. The original system was later replaced by a three-way version that included a heaver duty low-frequency driver, the large-format 375 driver, and a UHF ring radiator for heavier duty monitoring applications.

The mid 1960s also saw the development of JBL electronics. "Energizer" amplifiers based on Locanthi's "T-circuit" complementary topology were developed as free-standing units and were also mounted in the rear of both professional and consumer loudspeakers to create fully integrated systems. The D50SMS7 powered version can lay claim to being the first two-way powered studio monitor.

Another example of the synergy between JBL and the recording profession was the development of the first so-called bookshelf monitor system. When noted New York recording engineer and entrepreneur C. Robert Fine converted to 8-track recording in the late sixties, he needed eight small loudspeakers to be arrayed over the control room window for monitoring each track independently. His request to JBL was to make a rugged three-way design with a sonic signature as much like the Altec 604 as possible. The result was the 4310 monitor. Word of the new system spread quickly and sales soared.

By 1968 Thomas had given the go-ahead to form a Professional Division at JBL. A new four-digit model numbering system had been developed for an anticipated distribution arrangement with the Graybar Electric Company, one of the largest electrical suppliers in the country. That arrangement never materialized, and a decision was then made to launch the program directly.

The 4310 bookshelf monitor, originally designed for Fine Recording Company, New York City.

Fender-JBL joint ad from the 1960s. (Fender® is a registered trademark owned by Fender Musical Instruments Corporation and is used herein with express written permission. All rights reserved.)

George Augspurger, who is widely known today for his pioneering work in studio, control room, and monitor design, was instrumental in setting up the new division. In building a marketing base for its Pro division, JBL sought out younger professionals in the sound business, many of whom had risen through the ranks of the high-level music reinforcement industry. The company also identified significant professional sound dealers and brought them into the fold as well. Thomas had felt for some time that the company needed a new logo. As innovative as Gould's basic 1955 design was, it had become dated and its strength somewhat diluted over the years, largely through casual application.

A bold new company logo—the one we know today—was designed by Arnold Wolf and introduced in 1965. In 1967, Wolf's design received a Certificate of Award in the Graphic Arts Competition sponsored by the Printing Industries of America.

By 1969, Bill Thomas could look back over 20 years of remarkable leadership of JBL. On his watch the company had survived adversity and ultimately reached sales in the range of eight to nine million dollars annually.

The company had become unquestionably the world's most highly regarded maker of elegant furniture-type systems with professional-grade componentry. In the areas of music applications, tour sound reinforcement, and studio recording, the company was the acknowledged leader worldwide. All of this had been accomplished, surprisingly, with little serious competition. If there was any regret, it was the inability of the company to establish an important role in the motion picture market.

Thomas had reached the age of 54—too young to retire, perhaps, but maybe just the right age to move to Ojai, CA, to raise avocados and citrus and enjoy his growing collection of fine lithographs. The next chapter in JBL's history would be in the capable hands of Sidney Harman.

LE15A   LE8T

LE14C   LE5-2

Representative models in the LE-Series.

Logo for Thomas's subsidiary company,
Transducers, Incorporated.

The C50SMS7 system designed for Capitol Records in
Hollywood. It was subsequently renumbered 4320.

Compression driver assembly at Casitas. JBL, at the
height of the Thomas era, relied more on human
skills than modern manufacturing technology.

The Harman Era

Dr. Sidney Harman, Executive Chairman of the Board, Harman International Industries

In 1969 William Thomas sold JBL to the Jervis Corporation, a precursor of Harman International Industries (HII). Sidney Harman, President of Jervis, had been one of the younger pioneers in the high-fidelity movement, and his company, Harman Kardon, was credited with the concept and introduction of the mono receiver in 1954 and the stereo receiver four years later.

Harman's business philosophy emphasized innovative products, in-house manufacturing, responsive product development, a profound respect for music, and above all an open corporate structure with ongoing dialog with workers at all levels. Industrial designer Arnold Wolf was installed as company president, and Irving Stern, a successful Southern California manufacturer's representative, was named Executive Vice President of Marketing.

One of Harman's first orders of business was to analyze JBL's physical plant and related assets in detail. It was immediately apparent that the company needed more space. As it stood, the plant was a conglomeration of loosely attached buildings and sheds stretching along Casitas Avenue. Workflow was congested and inventory control was rudimentary. The machine shop was manned by skilled workers, but much of the machinery itself was pre-war vintage. The engineering department, headed by Bart Locanthi, had a number of excellent people who worked more or less independently of each other. The pace of product introduction at JBL had traditionally been slow and product development had been influenced accordingly.

Early on, Walter Goodman, President of the International Division of Jervis, had been assigned the task of analyzing JBL's international sales. Over relatively few years, he and Bruce Scrogin put together an effective group of distributors in key locations, principally Europe and the Far East.

One of the first important marketing opportunities for JBL was the beneficial exploitation of the highly successful 4310 monitor and the newly introduced "Century" L100 consumer system. The two systems were virtually identical in performance and underscored the fact that many recording engineers and producers routinely had 4310s—and its subsequent upgraded replacement 4311—as the core of their home systems. The company's message was, "You can hear music in your home the way that recording engineers heard it when they created it."

The marketing strategy had been carefully and successfully worked out by Irving Stern and marketing executive Larry Phillips, and the L100 became the company's all time best seller. In time, other matching loudspeaker pairs were created; the

Clark Kent.

The JBL 4310 is especially designed for mastering, control room installations, mixdown facilities, portable playback systems. It's full of good things like:
Wide range response. Full 90° dispersion for vertical or horizontal placement. Power handling capability, 50 watts program material.
Front panel controls for separate adjustment of presence and brilliance.
12-inch long-excursion low frequency loudspeaker, massive mid-frequency direct radiator, separate ultra-high frequency transducer.
Only available through Professional Audio Contractors.

© National Periodical Publications

Beneath this mild mannered charcoal gray exterior, is the finest compact studio monitor money can buy.
It should be. The JBL 4310 was developed with the enthusiastic assistance of leading recording engineers. (And they're the only ones who can buy it.)
Now, guess what else the professionals have been doing with the 4310's for the last two years. You're right. They've been taking them home, using them as bookshelf speakers.
That's why we decided to get even.

Supershelf.

It's the new JBL Century L100. It would be the finest professional compact studio monitor money could buy except it's not sold to studios. (If that sounds like the JBL 4310, there's a reason. They're twins.)
JBL started with a definition of sound. It's the sound the artist creates, the sound the microphone hears, the sound the recording engineer captures.
Then they added oiled walnut and a new dimensional grille that's more acoustically transparent than cloth but has a texture, a shape and

colors like Ultra Blue or Russet Brown or Burnt Orange.
Oh, yes. The JBL Century L100 is the only speaker you can buy with individual controls under the grille so that you can match the sound to the room—just the right presence, just the right brilliance.
And then they checked the rule book.
There's absolutely no law against professional sound looking beautiful.

James B. Lansing Sound, Inc. 3249 Casitas Avenue, Los Angeles 90039. A division of Jervis Corporation
Check No. 42 on Reader Service Card

The famous Clark Kent/Supershelf ad from the early 1970s, the heyday of the L100.

consumer L200 and L300 models were elegant, pricy versions respectively of the larger professional models 4320 and 4333. For the moment at least, JBL was working the same Lansing strategy of the mid 1930s, when both professional and consumer versions of the Iconic system were available.

The famous "Clark Kent/Supershelf" ad, created by the noted Keye/Donna/Pearlstein agency, stated this duality dramatically. The company also issued a well-received two-LP set called *Sessions*, which detailed the anatomy of a recording session and the role of JBL monitors in the studio creative environment.

At the time, JBL's consumer distribution was carefully monitored by the corporation. The typical JBL dealer was an independent mid- to high-end audio dealer who catered to a dedicated clientele and who did not sell JBL products below the manufacturer's stated list price, following the Fair Trade statutes of the day. If JBL was to gain market share it would have to introduce new lower-cost products into a far more competitive marketplace and with a larger dealer base.

Cover art for the *Sessions* double-LP set.

In the early 1970s the first major oil embargo brought attention to other changes that were in the wind. Major Japanese electronics companies were paying more attention to the US market and brought out excellent products that were reliable and reasonable in cost. At the same time, European manufacturers were streamlining their distribution channels and offering products that were attractive to the American market. JBL could see a gradual erosion of its core consumer dealer base and concluded that major changes in marketing strategy had to be made.

The low-cost Decade line, introduced in 1973 and 1974, was JBL's first attempt at combining the company's core values of authentic wood finish and cast-frame drivers with small-sized and relatively low-output sensitivity. While these systems performed well they were generally viewed as plain and uninteresting—but with price tags reflecting the company's higher manufacturing costs. It was not a promising direction for the company.

Beginning in the mid 1970s, the transducer engineering group embarked on a program of developing new mid- and high-frequency drivers, including dome tweeters, that would facilitate the design of systems with truly flat acoustical response. Related matters such as baffle topology, enclosure edge and corner detail, and dividing network sophistication were all reexamined and were implemented in a relatively short time. Products such as the L166 bookshelf system and the powered subwoofer-dual satellite L212 system were the first to take advantage of these measures and drew excellent reviews, both for sonic accuracy and excellent stereo imaging. Perhaps the domestic flagship product of this era was the Model L250, which was introduced in the early 1980s. The L250 was engineered by Greg Timbers, and Doug Warner of Warner Design was responsible for the elegant and functional visual aspects. Prior to this time, JBL consumer and professional products had been largely engineered by the same group; from this time onward, engineering activities began to diverge into two specialized entities.

From the very outset of the Harman era there had been a need for a new company facility. Planning for a company move had begun in the early 1970s, and in 1976 ground was broken for a new factory in Northridge, a Los Angeles suburb in the western part of the San Fernando Valley. For the first time, all of the company's manufacturing operations would occupy a single location.

Toward the late 1970s, civil unrest in Zaire interrupted the world's chief supply of cobalt, a major constituent in Alnico V magnetic material. The mines were flooded by rebels, creating a shortage that would last for years. Decades earlier, most of the world's loudspeaker manufacturers had made the switch to so-called ferrite magnets and as such were unaffected by the cobalt shortage. Ferrite magnets were low-cost and plentiful, but they could not directly be retrofitted into JBL's existing driver models. The result is that the entire JBL line of drivers, cone as well as compression types, had to be redesigned—an operation that JBL engineers accomplished in less than a year. While analyzing the basic nature of ferrite materials, JBL's engineers developed a new magnetic topology, Symmetrical Field Geometry (SFG™), which actually improved on the traditional performance parameters of both ferrite and JBL's previous Alnico V designs.

In 1977 Sidney Harman was appointed to the post of Under-Secretary of Commerce in the Carter administration. By custom, he had to divest himself of all corporate stock or otherwise put it into a blind trust, and as major stockholder in HII he sold the company to Beatrice Foods.

Beatrice was a very large corporation whose holdings went far beyond foodstuffs and included a wide variety of basic consumer goods. At the time of the sale, HII's holdings included, among others, Harman Kardon, JBL, Tannoy (UK), Ortofon (Denmark), and the Harman Automotive Division. In 1979 Harman left his government post and within a year had bought back JBL from Beatrice Foods. Harman's return was cause for virtual celebration at JBL.

Views of the 250Ti system.

Present headquarters of JBL Incorporated in Northridge, CA.

JBL and the Motion Picture Industry

Don Keele had joined JBL's engineering department in the late 1970s and had designed a remarkable family of so-called Bi-Radial® horns that provided uniform coverage in the frequency range from 500 Hz to about 16 kHz. As such, these horns could be electrically equalized to provide uniform response, both along their principal axis and in terms of their total power output. This is the definition of the term "uniform power response." When these horns were used in conjunction with low-frequency drivers operating in simple ported, direct radiating enclosures, the result was a full-range system that could deliver uniform direct field coverage over a wide angle, while at the same time delivering substantially uniform power into the diffuse (reflected) sound field of the theater.

Such a system had been developed, and a paper describing it was presented by amplifier and system innovator (and later JBL engineer) Mark Engebretson and John Eargle of JBL at the Los Angeles Audio Engineering Society Convention in May 1981. The paper session was held in the prestigious Goldwyn Theater at the Academy of Motion Picture Arts and Sciences in Beverly Hills, CA, and the system was demonstrated to a large audience that included a number of people from the technical side of the movie business.

SMPTE Journal, November 1982

Cinema Sound Reproduction Systems: Technology Advances and System Design Considerations

By Mark Engebretson and John Eargle

Today's state-of-the-art criteria for motion-picture sound reproduction may fall far short of meeting the demands of motion-picture audiences in five to ten years. Present-day A-chain capabilities far exceed the capabilities of motion-picture theater playback equipment, and the gap widens at an ever-increasing rate. The authors propose a quantum improvement in film-sound playback systems as a necessary means to gain significant improvements in sound quality in the motion-picture theater.

Presented on May 12, 1981, at the 69th Audio Engineering Society Technical Meeting in Los Angeles, CA, by Mark Engebretson, Advanced Technology Design, Van Nuys, CA, and John Eargle, James B. Lansing Sound, Northridge, CA. This paper was received on April 27, 1982. Copyright © 1982 by the Society of Motion Picture and Television Engineers, Inc.

Header for SMPTE Journal article on new motion picture loudspeakers.

During the following two years this system caused a stir in the motion picture industry. A big upsurge in the building of theaters in the country was underway, and Tomlinson Holman's THX program for theater certification at Lucasfilm was in the process of identifying the desired componentry for proper playback of films. Independent measurements of the JBL 4675 system components had shown that it met the THX standards in terms of coverage uniformity and distortion—matters that had long concerned George Lucas. In addition, the Motion Picture Academy had in early 1984 installed such a system in its Goldwyn Theater, largely at the recommendation of John Bonner, of Warner Hollywood Studios, and Daniel Ross of the Academy staff. These events marked the reintroduction of JBL into motion picture theaters worldwide, and the company remains the dominant player in that field today.

Company Diversification

In the mid 1980s the name of the company was changed from James B. Lansing Sound, Incorporated, to JBL Incorporated. The new name reflected what had long since become commonplace—the worldwide use of "JBL" to indicate both the company and its products. At the same time it was decided that JBL Consumer and Professional Divisions would become separate companies. Both marketplaces had grown along different paths and had diversified widely over the years. Growth prospects also justified separating many of the marketing and administrative support functions as well.

JBL Consumer's products fell into the categories of home audio, car audio, installation products, and the nascent field of home theater. The sales and marketing headquarters of JBL Consumer were moved to Woodbury, NY, while product engineering and manufacturing remained in Northridge. JBL Pro's products had broadened into the areas of fixed installation sound reinforcement, studio monitoring, musical instrument applications, portable systems, and high-level tour sound applications under the leadership of Ron Means.

Both major areas had needs for electronic products, and in the early years JBL had manufactured these as well. But as HII had grown and acquired a variety of other manufacturers that specialized in electronics, these products could now be economically produced by other companies under the same corporate umbrella.

Flagship Products for the Japanese Market

The Japanese have shown special reverence for JBL's products for many decades. As the story is told, the pre-war Japanese infatuation with early Western Electric systems of the 1930s was briefly transferred to Altec after the LMC acquisition took place. In the early 1950s, when JBL reintroduced the modernized version of the old WE 594 compression driver as the 375, the mantle was quickly transferred to JBL. Affluent Japanese have always been drawn to "big" systems such as the Hartsfield and Paragon and, when the larger 4300-Series monitors were introduced in the 1970s, they became the new favorites—particularly the model 4343 design.

In 1985, the Everest DD55000 system was introduced to the Japanese market.

The system used Keele's asymmetrical horns that, in a stereo configuration, allowed high frequencies to be cross-fired toward the listening area. This provided a stereo effect not unlike that of the Paragon, and the effective stereo "sweetspot" was greatly enlarged. During the Everest's introduction in Tokyo, demonstrations were made to groups as large as 50 persons—all of whom remarked that the stereo imaging was accurate and unambiguous. Subsequent Japanese models have been introduced at about five-year intervals since the Everest, each highlighting a new technical advantage, including reduced distortion in low-frequency drivers and the use of beryllium high-frequency diaphragms with response extending to 48,000 Hz. These special Japanese models all use fine furniture wood and other elegant visual details. Acoustically, they all make use of long-excursion low-frequency drivers in ported enclosures and horn-compression drivers for mid and high frequencies. In these regards they hark back to earlier designs of the 1950s, but also include many modern improvements, both in driver design and diaphragm materials as well as in dividing network topology.

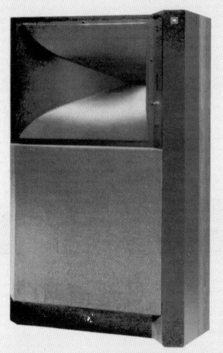

Everest DD55000   **K2 S9500**   **K2 S9800**

Flagship products for the Japanese market.

The Past 15 Years

During this period HII has acquired a diversified array of audio companies. On the consumer side, the list presently includes JBL Consumer, Harman Kardon, Infinity Systems, Lexicon Home Products, Mark Levinson, Audio Access, Revel, and Harman Becker Automotive Systems. Paul Bente is the president of JBL Consumer, which is a member of the Harman Consumer Group under the direction of president Gina Harman. Bernard Girod is the chief executive officer of the Corporation and Sidney Harman is the executive chairman.

The Harman Pro Group consists of JBL Professional, Crown, dbx, Soundcraft, AKG Acoustics, BSS, Studer, and Lexicon. A unifying element in this professional group is the proprietary HiQnet, a proprietary networking system introduced in 2005 for product from all companies in the group. John Carpanini is the president of JBL Professional, and Blake Augsburger is the president of the Harman Pro Group. Mr. Augsburger, former president of Crown International, succeeded Mark Terry (also a former JBL Pro president) as president of the Harman Pro Group in 2006.

Corporate Audio Research

In the early 1990s an HII corporate audio research division was established under the direction of Floyd Toole. In addition to fundamental research in acoustics, this activity provides a variety of psychoacoustical-based design and measurement services for the corporation at large. Many of these studies have led to new product areas as well as refinement of existing design philosophies. The facility is located at the Northridge Corporate Center.

The Synthesis® Systems

The introduction of the DVD during the mid 1990s led to the quick demise of the Laserdisc and diminished the influence of the VHS tape format. Many high-end audio dealers who thrived through the 1970s and 1980s found themselves becoming increasingly involved with high-end video and the seemingly unending progression of improvements in projection technology. The Synthesis® project was conceived at this time by JBL Consumer as a way of asserting JBL's dominant position in the motion picture arts and sciences and its translation into the home environment. A typical Synthesis system is targeted at an affluent user who can devote space in the home for a dedicated theater environment, and the audio systems themselves combine the best aspects of traditional professional and consumer technology.

In its fullest form, Synthesis provides performance that rivals that of state-of-the-art commercial theaters. Components include loudspeakers, electronics, room equalization, and various format control electronics. These systems are normally installed in dedicated spaces such as "media rooms" in modern residences and corporate facilities. High-performance video projection systems are also an important element in these installations.

A residential Synthesis installation with video projector lowered from ceiling.
Loudspeakers placed behind scrim at the sides and below the screen.

Technical Honors

In 1958, nine years after his death, James B. Lansing was awarded a posthumous citation by the Audio Engineering Society. The citation read "for his unique contributions to the original development of the Shearer theatre horn loudspeaker, and to the many electroacoustical devices which bear his name."

In March 2002, John Eargle, D.B. "Don" Keele, and Mark Engebretson—the three JBL engineers who had developed the original concept, design, and engineering of the modern constant-directivity, direct radiator style motion picture loudspeaker system—were given Scientific and Engineering awards for 2001 by the Academy of Motion Picture Arts and Sciences.

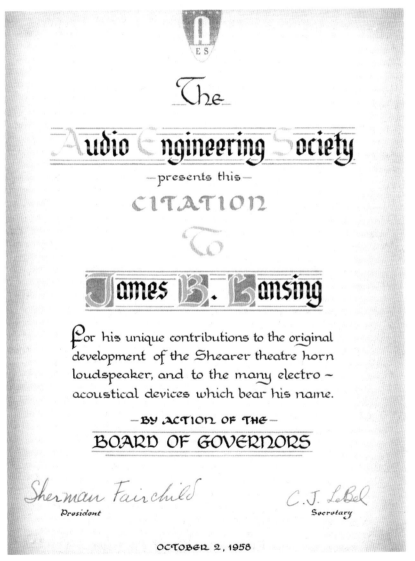

At the same ceremony, the Academy honored two additional JBL engineers, Bernard Werner and William Gelow, with Technical Achievement Awards for their work in the engineering and design of Filtered Array Technology™ and Screen Spreading Compensation™ as applied to JBL ScreenArray® systems. These were the first AMPAS technical awards given for loudspeaker developments since the award given for the Shearer-Lansing system in 1936.

In February 2005, JBL Professional received a Technical Grammy from the National Academy of Recording Arts and Sciences for 2004. The citation read "for continual mastery and innovation in concert, studio, cinema and broadcast sound and monitors to ensure exacting standards for the most accurate sonic experience."

A posthumous tribute to James B. Lansing. Courtesy Lois O'Neil

The Academy of Motion Pictures Arts and Sciences

2001 Scientific and Engineering Award

The Academy of Motion Pictures Arts and Sciences

2001 Technical Achievement Award

Citations to JBL engineering personnel in 2002 by the Academy of Motion Picture Arts and Sciences.

Technical Grammy awarded to JBL Professional in 2005.

Major Milestones in the Life of Lansing and JBL

1902   James B Lansing born in Illinois.

1927   Lansing Manufacturing Company founded in Los Angeles.

1934   Douglas Shearer of MGM heads team which designs first practical loudspeaker system for motion picture use. Lansing builds components for the system.

1936   Shearer-Lansing system awarded citation by the Academy of Motion Picture Arts and sciences.

1938   Lansing creates the "Iconic" two-way compact design—the first studio monitor.

1941   Lansing Manufacturing Company acquired by Altec Service Company.

1943   Lansing develops improved manufacturing methods, including flat wire milling and high-speed winding of ribbon wire voice coils.

         Lansing designs the 604 Duplex loudspeaker.

1944   Lansing and Hilliard redefine the state of the art for the motion picture theater with the A-4, dubbed Voice of the Theatre.

1946   Lansing founds a new company, James B. Lansing Sound, Incorporated, to pursue new directions in transducer and sound system design.

1947   JBL introduces the D130 15-inch loudspeaker, the first known use of a 4-inch flat wire voice coil in a cone transducer.

1949   James. B. Lansing dies; William Thomas becomes company president.

1954   JBL introduces the model 375 high-frequency compression driver. This was the first commercially available 4-inch diaphragm driver and achieved flat response to 9 kHz.

         JBL introduces a family of acoustic lenses developed by Locanthi.

         Model 075 high-efficiency high-frequency ring radiator introduced.

1955   Leo Fender incorporates the model D130 into his famous guitar amplifiers, signaling JBL's entry into the music reinforcement field.

1958   JBL introduces the Paragon stereophonic loudspeaker system, incorporating a cylindrical reflecting principle for superior stereophonic imaging in the home.

James B. Lansing posthumously awarded a Citation by Audio Engineering Society for "Contributions to Loudspeaker Design" at the New York Convention; family members are present to receive the award.

1962   JBL introduces the first two-way studio monitor using a high-frequency compression driver with acoustical lens.

1963   JBL introduces the LE8T, the industry's best known, single-cone full-range loudspeaker.

1965   JBL introduces the-"T-circuit" output configuration for high-performance solid-state amplifiers. The "Energizer" module version is mounted inside JBL loudspeaker systems, including the D50SMS7, creating the first two-way powered studio monitor.

1968   JBL introduces the 4310 three-way bookshelf monitor. This system, continued on as the 4311, lives on today as the 4312.

1969   Sidney Harman acquires JBL from William Thomas. Company embarks on a period of accelerated international growth through the Harman distribution companies.

        The L100, a consumer version of the 4311, is introduced, eventually reaching sales of 125,000 pairs during the 1970s.

1973   JBL introduces the expanded line of 4300-series monitors, including the industry's first four-way designs.

1976   JBL's monitors rank first in the US recording industry survey conducted by *Billboard* magazine.

1977   JBL moves to new location in Northridge, California.

1979   JBL introduced Symmetrical Field Geometry (SFG), a new ferrite-based magnetic structure with performance exceeding that of traditional Alnico V.

1981   Bi-Radial® monitors introduced. Building on the acoustical concept of flat power response, the 4400-series monitors quickly gain acceptance by the recording industry.

        L250 four-way consumer system introduced.

1982   The 4675 cinema system is introduced. It becomes the first power-flat cinema system to be approved by THX® for their theater certification program.

1983	Titanium is introduced as a diaphragm material in compression drivers.
	The model 4660 defined-coverage system is introduced. Based on Bi-Radial® technology, the system provides tailored coverage for speech application in rectangular spaces.
1984	Titanium dome tweeters are introduced into consumer products, providing superlative response to 27 kHz.
	UREI acquired by JBL, bringing their electronics design and manufacturing expertise to JBL's traditional line of loudspeaker components.
	The Academy of Motion Picture Arts and Sciences selects JBL components for the new system in the Samuel Goldwyn Theater.
1985	The Everest DD 55000 consumer system is selected by Japan's *Stereo Sound* as Product of the Year.
1989	The Directors Guild of America selects JBL components for the systems in Theaters 1 and 2 in their Hollywood headquarters building.
	JBL develops VGC (Vented Gap Cooling) for raising the thermal power limits of low-frequency transducers.
1991	JBL's K-2 loudspeaker system is selected by Japan's *Stereo Sound* as Product of the Year.
	JBL develops the 1400Nd, the first neodymium high-power low-frequency driver for professional applications.
1992	JBL introduces a new large-format lower-midrange compression driver with matching horns.
1993	JBL develops new "rapid flare" low-distortion compression driver and matching family of horns.
	JBL Synthesis® consumer products for high-end home video introduced.
1995	JBL introduces EON® molded enclosure, integrated powered, portable loudspeakers. These systems also include Differential Drive® transducer technology and TTMS Total Thermal Management System design.
1997	JBL introduces the LSR (Linear Spatial Reference) family of studio monitor loudspeakers.
2000	JBL introduces VerTec line array systems, including new driver technology for MF and HF elements.
	James B. Lansing inducted posthumously into the Consumer Electronics Association Hall of Fame for

2001   JBL's K2S9800 consumer system capable of 48 kHz response introduced in Japan.

2002   Three JBL engineers given a Science and Engineering Awards by the Academy of Motion Picture
        Arts and Sciences for development of constant HF coverage ported LF systems for cinema playback.
        Two JBL engineers given Technical Achievement Awards by the Academy of Motion Picture Arts
        and Sciences for development of JBL ScreenArray® system.

2005   JBL Professional awarded a Technical Grammy by the National Academy of Recording
        Arts and Sciences.

Chapter 2: Engineering and Technology at JBL

JBL has had a long identification with innovation in transducer design, manufacturing methods, systems concepts, and analytical tools for the users of its products. The company routinely publishes Technical Notes in support of professional users, and no audio company publishes more in the way of product manuals for both consumer and professional users.

In this chapter we highlight many of the developments from 1946 to the present. In the early days, the company existed primarily on a legacy that Jim Lansing had brought with him from five years as vice president of Engineering at the Altec Lansing Corporation. He clearly saw the need for developing a new line of transducers based on four-inch diameter diaphragms and voice coils. He died before all of these projects were completed, but his determination was carried on by William Thomas.

It is fitting then that the early items to be discussed here concentrate on transducers and their associated hardware, as these gave the new company an immediate advantage over its competition in commercial problem solving. At the same time, Thomas's insistence on quality industrial design gave the company an image and immediate cachet in a high-end high-fidelity market that was in its beginning phases. The look and feel of heavy castings and fine machining have always served JBL well and underscored the basic technology employed.

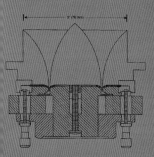

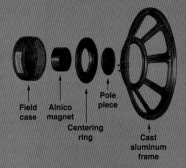

Field case Alnico magnet Centering ring Pole piece Cast aluminum frame

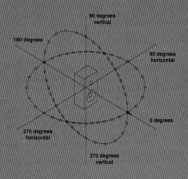

D130 Full-Range Cone Transducer

In August 1947 Lansing contacted Arnold Engineering Company of Chicago for advice on advanced magnetic materials for use in a new 15-inch (380 mm) cone transducer. What Lansing had in mind was a model with a stiff, light-weight cone, high-output capability, and low distortion that would be suitable for use in conventional ported systems as well as in low-frequency horn applications. He saw these specific applications as key to the growth of his new company.

The D130 was not the first transducer to make use of a 4-inch (100 mm) edge-wound aluminum ribbon voice coil, but it was the first of its size and power-handling capability to do so. Its primary design elements were:

1. Curvilinear felted paper cone for minimum breakup at high excursions
2. Low moving mass
3. High magnetic flux density (12,000 gauss)
4. Rear cone venting to eliminate audible air turbulence
5. Cast aluminum frame to assure rigidity and mounting integrity
6. Aluminum voice coil dome to radiate high frequencies

A photograph of an early D130, very likely built in the San Marcos facility, is shown at **A**, and an exploded view is shown at **B**. A later version using a cast iron pot structure is shown at **C**, and its on-axis response is shown at **D**. Note that the response extends out to the 2 to 4 kHz range, making it ideal for many musical instrument applications.

A. An early D130.

B. Exploded view of D130.

C. A later version of a D130 with a cast iron pot structure.

D. Typical on-axis response of a D130.

A.

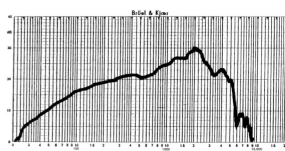

D.

C.

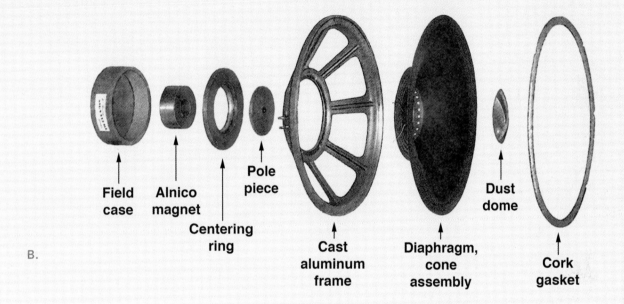

Field case　**Alnico magnet**　**Pole piece**　**Dust dome**

Centering ring

B.

Cast aluminum frame　**Diaphragm, cone assembly**　**Cork gasket**

In one form or another, the D130 has remained in the JBL catalog to this day. It revolutionized high-level sound reinforcement and was adopted early on as the loudspeaker of choice for electronic musical instrument applications. Leo Fender was looking for a suitable cone transducer that would complement guitar amplifier designs. He found the answer in the D130, and eventually Fender sold a version of the D130 under his own name.

The Ultra High Frequency (UHF) Ring Radiator

With the rapid growth of the high fidelity movement in the early fifties, William Thomas, President of JBL, initiated an engineering study of high-output, low-distortion sound-radiating principles. This study led to the development of the model 075 ring radiator, an integral motor structure and annular horn. The 075 is shown at A and its radiating characteristics are shown at B. The sensitivity of the unit was a remarkable 102 dB at one meter for power input of one watt. The power rating of 40 watts indicated that the unit could deliver acoustical output sufficient to fill a large room with high frequency power at moderate input levels.

When the JBL Professional division was formed, the 075 was given the model number 2402. In succeeding years three additional versions with different radiation patterns were introduced and are shown at C. The motor structure remains essentially the same, but the horn sections have been modified to produce different radiation patterns. A section view of the entire 2402 structure is shown at D.

In addition to its intended high fidelity and studio monitor uses, clusters of ring radiators are often flown overhead in discotheques for wide-area blanket coverage of high frequencies that can be heard well over the high noise levels in those spaces.

A. Photo of an 075 ring radiator.

B. Polar response of an 075 ring radiator.

C. Models 2403, 2404, and 2405 ring radiators.

D. Section view of an 075 ring radiator.

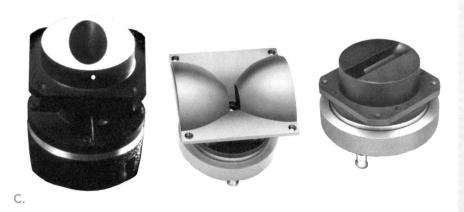

C.

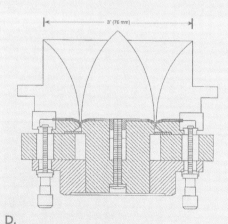

D.

A.

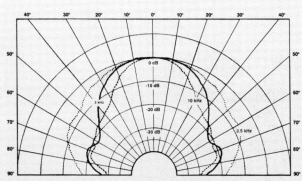

B.

Polar response of the 2402H in the horizontal plane, measured with ⅓-octave band pink noise in a free-field environment. The curves were traced by an automatic recorder. Power fed to the 2402H was adjusted to provide the same 0 dB reference for each curve.

The 375 High Frequency Compression Driver

It was always Jim Lansing's desire to design and build a compression driver with a 4-inch (100-mm) diameter diaphragm. The basic format he had in mind was that of the Western Electric 594, which had first been used for experimental sound transmission studies at Bell Telephone Laboratories in 1933 and 1934. Lansing's sketches (shown at A) indicate that he had seriously considered taking on such a project, but it wasn't until five years after his death that the company introduced a model in 1954.

Fueled by the development of motion picture stereo, the engineering costs of the JBL model 375 were shared by JBL, Ampex Corporation, and Westrex Corporation. A photo of the 375 (with cover removed) is shown at B, and a section view is shown at C.

In keeping with the needs of the motion picture industry at that time, response beyond 9 kHz was not necessary, and the on-axis response of the driver, mounted on an Ampex 90-degree horn, indicates how well the design goals had been met (response curve shown at D). The 375 was introduced into the JBL Professional line as the model 2440. Later, the Ampex 90-degree horn was acquired by JBL and became the model 2350.

B.

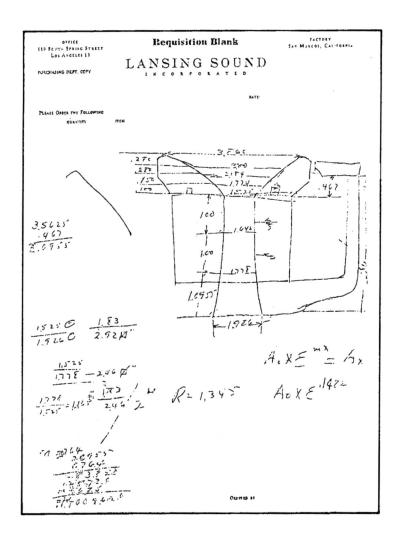

A.

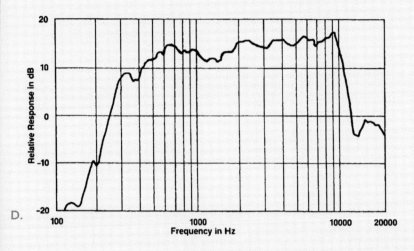

D.

A. Lansing's engineering notes from the late 1940s.

B. Model 375 with cover removed.

C. Section view of 375 driver.

D. On-axis frequency response of the 375 driver mounted on 2350 radial horn.

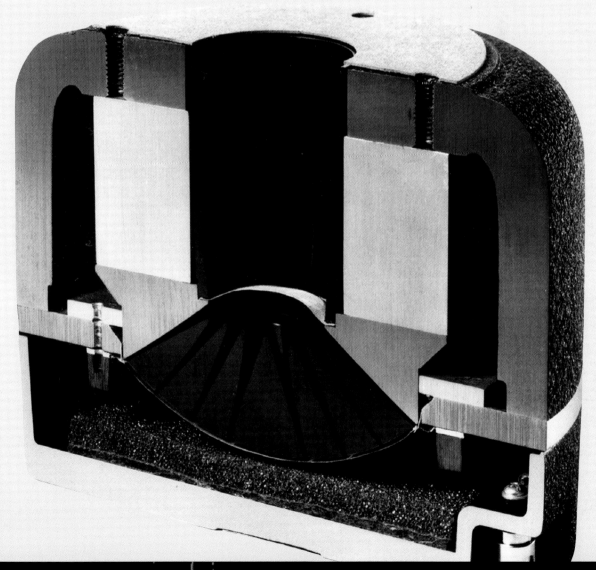

C.

The Acoustic Lens

While the Ampex cinema systems made use of traditional radial horns for high frequency coverage, the acoustic lens was adopted by Westrex as the high-frequency choice for its international export market. Early work on acoustical lenses had been carried out by Kock and Harvey at Bell Telephone Laboratories, but the first commercialization of the principle was carried out in the early fifties by John Frayne of Westrex and Bart Locanthi, senior consultant to JBL at the time.

Over the decade of the 1950s a number of acoustic lenses were developed. A group photograph of these is shown at A. There were basically two kinds: slant plate and perforated plate. Both designs provided the necessary shorter central path for sound to radiate through, and this ensured that sound waves would be launched from the mouth of the horn at a fairly wide angle. The analogy with an optical lens is shown at B.

The horizontal slant plate designs widened the radiation pattern only in the horizontal plane, while the perforated plate designs widened the radiation pattern uniformly. For applications in very large theaters, Westrex specified a correspondingly large version of the perforated plate design, as shown at C.

A. JBL family of slant plate and perforated plate lenses.

B. Principle of the acoustical lens.

C. HL94 perforated plate lens and Westrex C5070 theater system.

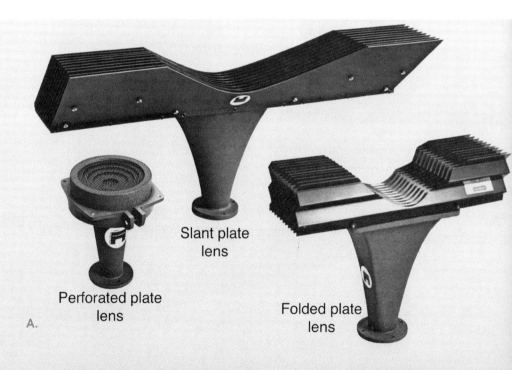

Slant plate lens

Perforated plate lens

Folded plate lens

A.

C.

OPTICAL

Diverging light beams

Concave
lens

Parallel light beams

ACOUSTICAL

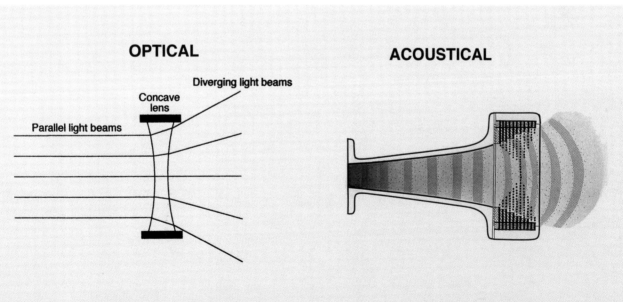

B.

The LE8T

The full-range LE8T was a truly unique JBL product of the mid-fifties. This transducer had a fairly thin felted paper cone, coated on front and back with a damping compound called Aquaplas® to give it the required mass, stiffness, and internal damping. The short aluminum ribbon voice coil was totally immersed in a deep magnetic field, ensuring that cone excursions at high drive levels would be linear. The 2-inch aluminum dust dome, cemented directly to the voice coil former, was selectively damped and permitted extended on-axis high frequency response out to 12 – 15 kHz. A view of the transducer is shown at A, and a cutaway view is shown at B. A typical application is shown at C, and a comparison of typical on-axis and power response is shown at D. Edmund May was responsible for the successful design of the LE8T.

THE TRIMLINE 54....

NEW PASSIVE LOW FREQUENCY RADIATOR GIVES FULL, TRUE BASS IN LESS THAN A CUBIC FOOT OF SPACE!

C.

LE 8

8-inch passive radiator

A. Photo of LE8T.

B. Cutaway view of LE8T.

C. A typical application of the LE8T.

D. Frequency response of the LE8T (dashed curve shows response at 45° off-axis).

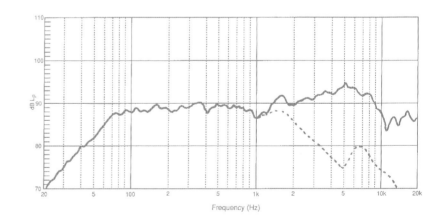

D.

A.

B.

A CUBIC FOOT
OF SPACE!

LE 8

8-inch passive

The 4300-Series Studio Monitors

A.

Prior to the early sixties, the Altec Lansing 604 or British Tannoy Dual Concentric coaxial loudspeakers had been considered the only professional choices for modern recording studio applications around the world. During this period, Altec Lansing briefly discontinued the 604, substituting for it the cost-reduced model 605. As a result of this, Capitol Records, whose west coast pressing plant was just down the street from JBL's Fletcher Drive plant, approached JBL regarding new monitoring concepts. By that time, JBL's dedication to 4-inch voice coils and general attention to design excellence were well established enough to merit such an inquiry from a major record label. Ed Uecke, VP of engineering for Capitol Records, contacted Bart Locanthi, who by that time had become VP of engineering at JBL. Between them, a broad design statement for a new monitor evolved, consisting of the following features:

1. A dedicated enclosure whose volume and tuning frequency were targeted for the new JBL LE-series of low frequency transducers
2. Use of a small format slant plate acoustical lens mounted on a short high frequency horn
3. Dividing network response tailored for flat on-axis response
4. Availability in either utility gray or oiled walnut enclosures.

B.

C.

The new C50SMS7 monitor (later renamed 4320) was a great hit, and Capitol's parent company, EMI, roundly adopted the concept. (It is estimated that, at that time, there were about 250 monitor channels in EMI recording and remix installations worldwide.) In addition, the availability of the 4320 in an oiled walnut enclosure brought it out of the control room and into executive suites and homes of many recording artists.

Over the next 15 or so years, various additions to the line were made, including the 4325, 4333-Series (three-way), 4340-Series (four-way), and the mammoth 4350 model. A photo of the original C50SMS7 is shown at A. A group shot of mid-1970s monitors is shown at B, and a view of the 4350, grilles removed, is shown at C.

A. Original JBL C50SMS7.

B. JBL 4300-Series monitors, mid-1970s.

C. JBL 4350 4-way monitor.

JBL's T-Circuit Amplifiers

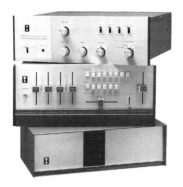

B.

In the mid 1960's, Bart Locanthi designed a unique topology for solid-state power amplifier output circuitry. Circuit details are shown at **A**, and it is quite clear where the designation "T" comes from. The design approach was used in a number of JBL consumer receivers, along with separate preamplifier-amplifier combinations, as shown at **B**.

Some of the earliest examples of powered monitor systems date from this period. Front and back views of the model D50SMS7 are shown at **C**, and a close-up view of the amplifier is shown at **D**. Whether for professional or consumer use, frequency shaping was introduced into these various models to produce flat system on-axis response.

At the time, the T-circuit was considered a major step forward in output circuit topology, influencing many designers of the day. Despite the many changes that have been made in circuit design over succeeding decades, the early JBL electronics, especially in the Orient, remain collector's items and command very high prices.

A. Basic T-circuit schematic.

B. JBL consumer products using T-circuit.

C. Front and rear views of JBL D50SMS7 system.

D. Detail of SE400-Series Energizer amplifier.

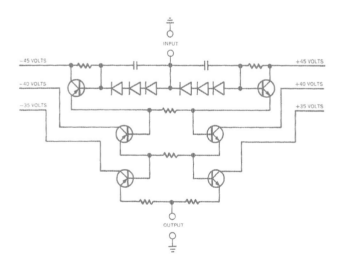

A.

C.

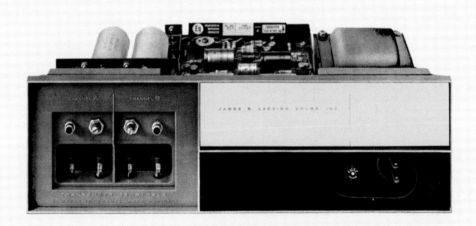

D.

Symmetrical Field Geometry (SFG) Magnetic Structures

In the mid 1970s civil unrest in Zaire resulted in the closing of the country's cobalt mines, severely impacting the availability of this crucial element worldwide. The high-end loudspeaker industry was particularly affected, inasmuch as it had evolved over 30 years of ready availability of Alnico (aluminum-nickel-cobalt) materials. For many companies, various ferrite-ceramic magnetic materials were in common use, primarily because of their lower costs relative to Alnico. JBL had not adopted ferrites due to their inherent tendency to exhibit magnetic flux modulation and consequent distortion.

But in this case the company was forced to consider it as the only practical approach. Over the course of about two years the entire line of JBL's transducers was redesigned with ferrite magnets, but only after a research program that proved that this material could perform as well as, or in some cases better than, Alnico. The result of JBL's research was the development of Symmetrical Field Geometry (SFG).

There are two central design elements in SFG. The first is the use of an undercut polepiece, which allows the fringe magnetic flux field at the gap to be symmetrical, top and bottom. The other element is the very low-resistance aluminum flux shorting ring at the base of the polepiece, which creates a counter-flux counteracting the flux modulation.

A section view of JBL's older Alnico motor structure is shown at A, and a new SFG structure is shown at B. The new structure is bigger and heavier, neither of which is a practical advantage. However, an examination of the distortion performance of equivalent transducers shown at C indicates exceptional performance for the ferrite SFG version. In this example we are using identical moving systems, both driven at the same power input level.

A. Traditional JBL Alnico structure.

B. JBL ferrite SFG structure.

C. Distortion in Alnico V and SFG systems.

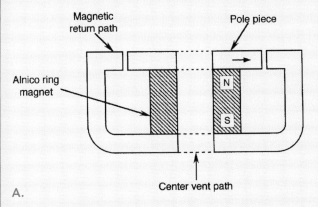

Magnetic return path

Pole piece

Alnico ring magnet

N

S

Center vent path

A.

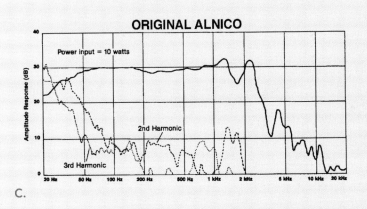

ORIGINAL ALNICO

Power input = 10 watts

Amplitude Response (dB)

2nd Harmonic

3rd Harmonic

20 Hz   50 Hz   100 Hz   200 Hz   500 Hz   1 kHz   2 kHz   5 kHz   10 kHz   20 kHz

C.

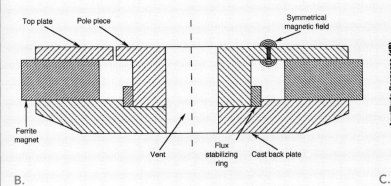

Top plate   Pole piece

Symmetrical magnetic field

Ferrite magnet

Vent

Flux stabilizing ring

Cast back plate

B.

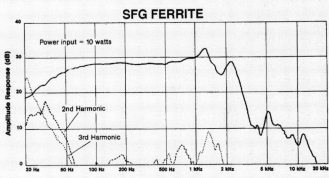

SFG FERRITE

Power input = 10 watts

Amplitude Response (dB)

2nd Harmonic

3rd Harmonic

20 Hz   50 Hz   100 Hz   200 Hz   500 Hz   1 kHz   2 kHz   5 kHz   10 kHz   20 kHz

C.

Symmetrical Field Geometry (SFG) Magnetic Structures

63

The JBL Bi-Radial Constant Coverage Horns

When D. B. Keele joined the JBL engineering staff in the mid 1970s, he brought with him a vast body of transducer/horn design knowledge as well as keen analytical skills. Building on his earlier work, he developed an algorithm for computing horn dimensions required for maintaining target vertical and horizontal –6-dB coverage angles over designated frequency ranges. Traditional horn hardware at that time could provide adequate coverage angles in either the vertical or horizontal planes, but not simultaneously in both planes.

The concern for uniform coverage devices had been raised by members of both manufacturing and acoustical consulting groups after years of specifying from a very long list of individual components for sound reinforcement array design. This general concern eventually became known as the "flat power response" concept, and it virtually reinvented and redefined the scope of both speech and music reinforcement. Every segment of professional audio—from music recording, cinema applications, and high-level music and speech reinforcement—to home hi-fi, were to be influenced by this concept. The new Keele horns were designated Bi-Radial, inasmuch as their mouth boundaries were defined by the radius from the compression driver and the radius from the diffraction opening. These relationships are shown at A. The beamwidth plots of a JBL 2360A Bi-Radial horn are shown at B, exhibiting remarkably uniform pattern control from 500 Hz to 12.5 kHz.

Three large format Bi-Radial horns are shown at C, and a smaller studio monitor version with 100°-by-100° coverage is shown at D. Keele's Bi-Radial designs are covered by US Patent 4,308,932.

C.

A.

Short radius

Long radius

TOP VIEW   SIDE VIEW

A. Top and side views of a
Bi-Radial horn.

B. Beamwidth data for JBL 2360A
Bi-Radial horn.

C. Family of JBL 2360-Series
Bi-Radial horns.

D. JBL Model 2344 Bi-Radial horn.

D.

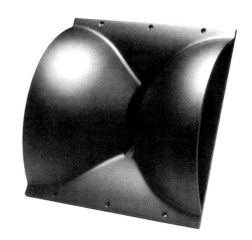

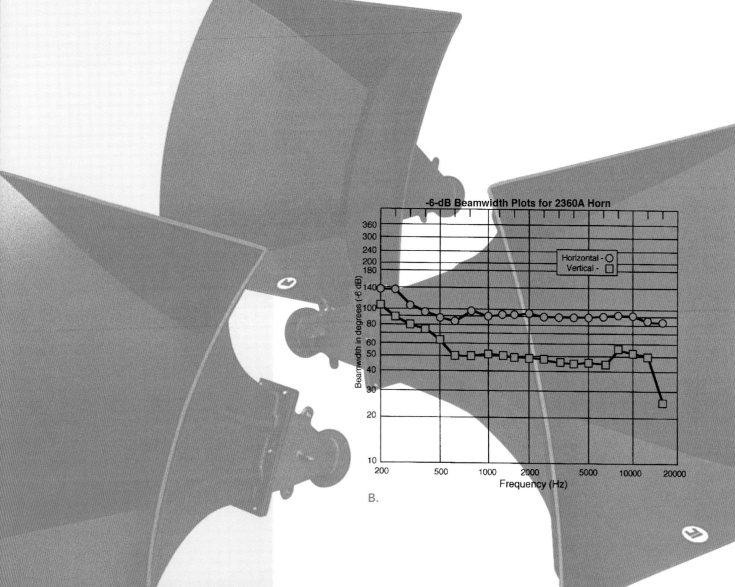

-6-dB Beamwidth Plots for 2360A Horn

Horizontal - ◯
Vertical - ▢

Beamwidth in degrees (-6 dB)

Frequency (Hz)

B.

Improvements in Compression Drivers: The Diamond Surround and Titanium

A. Top and side section view of a half-roll surround.

B. Top and side section views of a "diamond" surround.

C. Response of half-roll (2440) and diamond surround (2441) diaphragms on JBL 2350 horn.

D. Raw drawn titanium diaphragm with diamond surround.

Historically, JBL's large-format drivers used half-roll outer surrounds, as shown at A. Mechanically, the half-roll surround boosts high frequencies up to its resonance frequency of 9 kHz, and this was sufficient in the early days. In the early 1980s, JBL engineers Fancher Murray and Howard Durbin developed a new surround profile that permitted extended driver operation well beyond the previous resonance limitation. The reticulated design, shown at B, resembled a string of diamonds—thus the name *diamond surround*.

The new surround works on the following principle: when finely embossed patterns are used as surround elements, their individual resonances are distributed and extend beyond 20 kHz. By comparison, a half-roll surround exhibits a much lower resonance. These differences can clearly be seen at C, where we show the response of two earlier aluminum diaphragm drivers, one with a traditional surround and the other with the new design. Clearly, a gentle electrical boost in the response of the 2441 will enable smooth response beyond 20 kHz, whereas no amount of boost will enable the 2440 to perform beyond 9 kHz.

Shortly after this development, JBL was the first to develop a method of forming titanium diaphragms, and a new generation of advanced compression drivers, large and small, came into being. Titanium is stiffer than aluminum and less prone to mechanical fatigue over long operating periods. A typical 4-inch titanium driver carries a rating of 100 watts (continuous program) in the range above 500 Hz and a rating of 150 watts in the range over 1 kHz. For long-term operation in high-level music reinforcement and cinema action films, titanium clearly has the advantage over other materials. A photo of a freshly drawn titanium diamond diaphragm is shown at D.

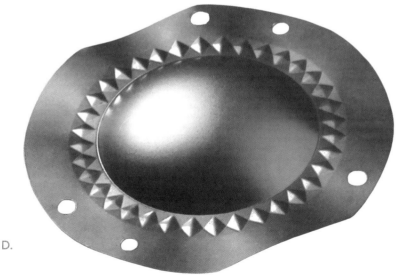

D.

Half-roll surround

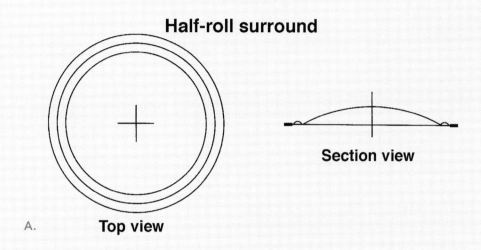

Section view

A.   Top view

"Diamond" surround

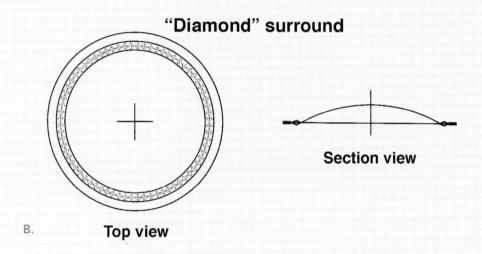

Section view

B.   Top view

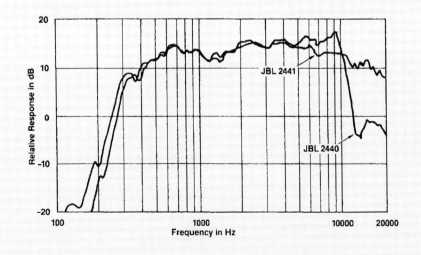

JBL 2441

JBL 2440

C.

Coherent Wave™ Phasing Plug

In traditional phasing plug design, the path lengths from the center of the diaphragm are slightly longer than those from the outer annular slits. For many years the industry has ignored this consideration inasmuch as the discrepancies in distances involved were small with regard to the wavelengths of sound, even at the highest frequencies. During the early 1980s, JBL engineer Fancher Murray designed a phasing plug version in which all annular paths are of equal length. The design is most effective when the diaphragm exhibits pistonic, or near-pistonic, motion, since that motion will be developed as a plane wave directly at the input to the following horn or waveguide over the entire frequency passband.

Section views of traditional and Coherent Wave phasing plugs are shown at **A**. The photograph at **B** shows a system cutaway view with both horn and driver details in the upper portion. (The lower portion of the photograph at **B** also shows a cutaway view of the model 1400PRO, the first low frequency professional driver in the industry to use a neodymium magnet structure.)

Traditional Phasing Plug Design

Coherent Wave Phasing Plug Design

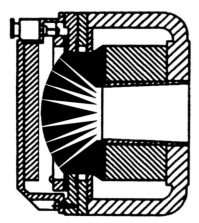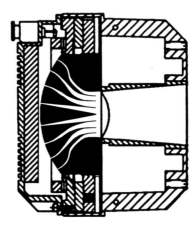

A. Section views of standard and Coherent Wave phasing plugs.

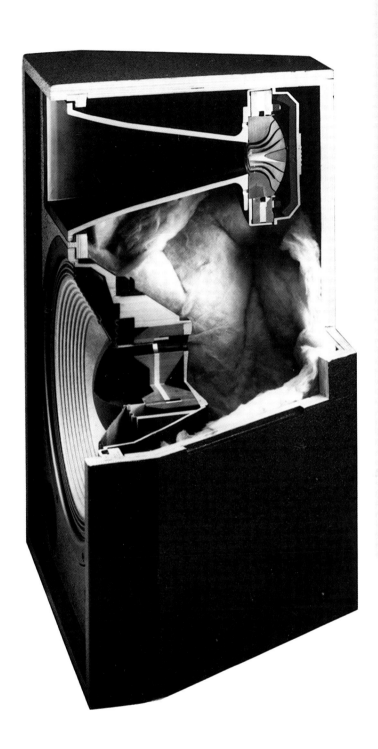

B. Section view of a system using Coherent Wave phasing plug.

The Bi-Radial® Monitor Loudspeakers

After nearly 15 years of building three- and four-way large-format monitor systems, JBL made a major decision in the early 1980s to revisit two-way systems.

There were a number of reasons for doing this:
1. The rise of digital recording had impressed on recording engineers the need for absolute time domain precision throughout the frequency range, and two-way systems vastly simplified this design goal.
2. The "flat power response" concept was in harmony with trends of the day in control room layout and acoustical design, in which boundary absorption coefficients were essentially uniform from 250 Hz upward. The use of power-flat systems in such spaces guaranteed a good match between on-axis and reflected sound power over a broadened listening zone.
3. Most importantly, JBL had the hardware necessary to carry out this project: low distortion transducers and Bi-Radial horn components.

The models 4430 and 4435, shown at A, were introduced in the early 1980s essentially as floor-standing models, capable of being flushed into the listening space if necessary. The striking appearance of the high frequency horn was not to be hidden from view, and these systems very likely led to the current trend of doing away with grille cloth, exposing the essential acoustical elements for what they actually are.

A side section view of the model 4430 is shown at B, and the vertical "launch angle" is approximately ten degrees above the on-axis position, which is ideal for floor placement of these systems.

Horizontal and vertical beamwidth curves for the 4430 are shown at C, along with the overall DI (directivity index). With the singular exception of the dip at 1 kHz (due to the simultaneous radiation of two vertically displaced sources), the angular coverage is remarkably uniform from 500 Hz to 10 kHz. The close tracking of directivity index and angular coverage curves indicates the uniformity of system power response. The square wave response of the model 4425, shown at D, gives an excellent indication of the time domain performance of these systems.

A. Views of the JBL 4430 and 4435 Bi-Radial monitors.

B. Time coherence in the Bi-Radial monitors.

C. Directivity and beamwidth plots for Bi-Radial monitors.

D. Square wave response of 4425 monitor at 365 Hz.

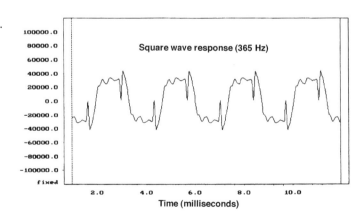

D.

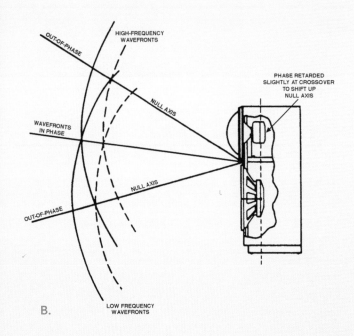

B.

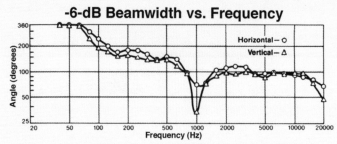

-6-dB Beamwidth vs. Frequency

Horizontal — ○
Vertical — △

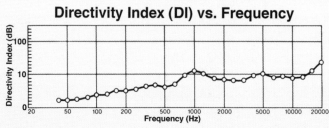

Directivity Index (DI) vs. Frequency

C.

A.

The 4675 Motion Picture System

Since the beginning of motion picture sound in the late 1920s, behind-the-screen loudspeakers were designed for maximum acoustical output with relatively modest power input. This led in time to the development of the Oscar-winning Shearer-Lansing system in the 1930s and the subsequent development of the Altec Lansing Voice of the Theatre® systems in the early 1940s. These systems were large, and made use of horn loading throughout their frequency range. They became symbolic of "movie sound" worldwide, and for nearly four decades they dominated the cinema market.

These systems represented the best technology available at the time of their invention, and this advantage continued unquestioned until the early 1980s. At that time the industry began to see the improvements in low frequency transducer design that had been brought about by the demands of high level concert sound reinforcement. These new transducers handled far more input power than their predecessors, and power amplifier design had kept pace with these improvements. In addition, there was the growing concern for flat power response in loudspeakers.

Although John Hilliard of Altec had hinted at such improvements as early as 1969, it was in the seminal paper by Engebretson and Eargle (1982) that clear technical roadmaps were presented for the design of these new cinema loudspeaker systems. The new designs had three supreme advantages over the older approach: they were smaller, performed better, and cost less than the previous systems.

The old theater technology (as typified by the Altec A-4) is shown at A, and the new technology is shown at B. Both systems have the same number of transducers, and the on- and off-axis response of the new system is much more uniform. A photograph of the JBL model 4675 is shown at C, and one of the earliest installations (Motion Picture Academy, 1984) is shown at D. Here, due to the size of the Goldwyn Theater, each screen channel has been supplemented with an additional low frequency unit operating below 200 Hz.

A. Older technology.

B. Newer technology.

C. Photo of JBL 4675 cinema system.

D. An early installation of 4675 systems, with added low frequency units. ("Academy Award" and "Oscar" image ©AMPAS®)

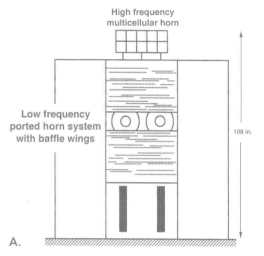

High frequency multicellular horn

Low frequency ported horn system with baffle wings

108 in.

A.

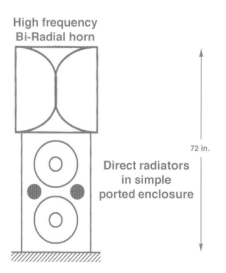

High frequency Bi-Radial horn

72 in.

Direct radiators in simple ported enclosure

B.

D.

C.

The JBL L250 and its Progeny

Unquestionably, the L250 is the longest-lived JBL Consumer loudspeaker system since the Paragon. Introduced in the early 1980s, it was the engineering brainchild of Greg Timbers, long-time JBL engineer. The elegant, warm industrial design was carried out by Douglas Warner in JBL's then-standard oiled walnut finish. Typical L250 response is shown at A.

The first embodiment of the L250 used the LE5 5-inch diameter midrange driver topped off by a 1-inch diameter phenolic dome tweeter with an aluminum coating. The two lower range drivers were the noted LE14 and an 8-inch midbass unit known as the 108H. The network topology was a straight-forward first-order design, with several conjugate sections to flatten the impedance characteristics. The choice of crossover frequencies, along with the felicitous boundary conditions of the enclosure, resulted in uniform on-axis response along with a monotonically rising directivity characteristic with increasing frequency. The result was clearly JBL's best expression of non-horn design principles, coupled with the company's traditional robust output capability. At the same time, a subwoofer, the model B460, was co-marketed with the L250, although it was more of an afterthought than an essential element.

By the mid 1980s a number of changes were made: a new titanium tweeter replaced the original phenolic model, and a new 5-inch midrange with a polypropylene cone was introduced. These new transducers contributed to greater clarity, and suitable network modifications were made. Boundary conditions for the drivers remained the same, and the overall result was a new lease on life for what was already a very successful system. This version, the 250Ti, is shown in an oiled walnut finish at B.

A. Amplitude and impedance plots for L250 system
   (ground plane measurements).

B. JBL 250Ti, with and without grille.

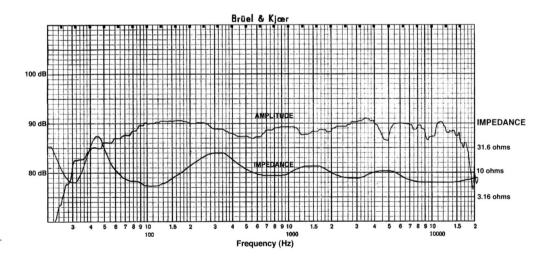

A.

B.

Over many years there have been numerous re-introductions of the system, including the Limited Edition, Classic, and Jubilee, this last version employing a "charge coupled linear definition dividing network." A casual glimpse at the Internet shows that the system is still very much alive.

Defined Coverage Horns

JBL engineer D. B. Keele introduced the defined coverage concept during the early 1980s. Heretofore, all horns had been designed to have a given vertical coverage angle and a given horizontal coverage angle. Keele's design provided for a fixed vertical coverage angle with two horizontal coverage angles, one near-field and the other far-field. Such a horn could be used for more precise coverage of rectangular seating spaces by providing a wide coverage angle toward the front, along with a narrow coverage angle as seen by the horn foreshortened toward the back of the space.

A photo of the JBL model 4660 system is shown at A. The view is as seen from the front, and the wide coverage portion of the system is seen at the back of the system (bottom of figure), showing a relatively wide horn mouth. The narrow mouth portion at front of the horn is aimed toward the rear of the seating area. A perspective view shown at B makes these relationships clear.

The seating floor, as seen from the horn's position, is shown in the left part of C. The actual family of measured coverage limits is shown at the right part of C. Here, you can clearly see that the coverage isobars are very close match to the outline of the actual seating space. Such systems as this allow a single device to be specified for speech reinforcement in many spaces. Using conventional radiating devices, a pair of horns would normally be called for.

Defined coverage horns are used in some of JBL's most advanced systems for motion picture applications. The design is covered by US Patent 4,580,655.

A. Photo of JBL 4660 system.

B. Oblique view of 4660 coverage limits.

C. 4660 coverage isobars as seen from the system's location.

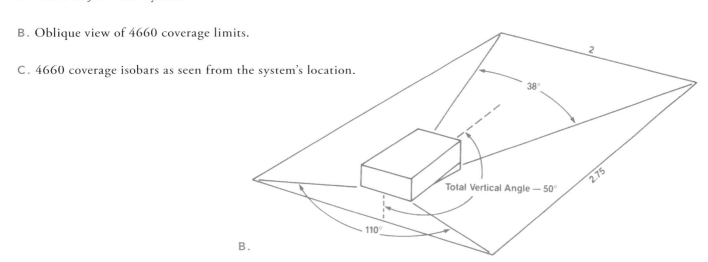

B.

A.

View of floor from horn

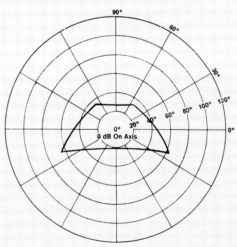

Coverage limits at 4 kHz

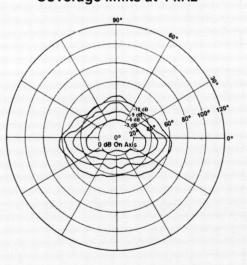

C.

JBL's Central Array Design Program (CADP)

With the rise of the personal computer in the early 1980s, engineers were quick to write complex acoustical design programs that took advantage of the speed of calculation these machines permitted. What was sorely lacking at the time was any degree of sophisticated graphics capability. Most of the everyday problems of sound system layout and calculation of acoustical levels at various listening positions were primarily determined using physical templates and overlays, and the notion of a personal computer program that could accomplish this task was little more than a dream to engineers. JBL's CADP was the first breakthrough in this area.

The primary calculation in sound system layout is shown at A. Here, we have a typical horn loudspeaker element positioned overhead, aimed downward toward a listening plane. We energize the loudspeaker, and our goal is to determine the direct field level at any position on the listening plane. The most difficult task is to determine the horn's polar pattern loss in the specific direction we are interested in. Given the horn's location, its orientation, and its power feed, the program, written in Microsoft Basic, determined a number of "readout positions" on the listening plane and proceeded to calculate the actual direct field levels at each position. For a typical seating plan reproduced on the computer screen, the number of readout positions was in the range of 100 to 150, far more than the engineer would ever have found the time to carry out manually.

Further program modules were based on acoustical input data and provided direct-to-reverberant ratios and estimates of speech intelligibility. Typical readouts for a cruciform shaped house of worship are shown at B. A graphics module provided views of loudspeaker component layout, as shown at C. By today's standards, the program was slow, and the graphic printouts were primitive. It was however a giant step in the right direction. Later modifications of the program made better use of advanced screen and printer graphics as well as more complex design modules.

A printout from a later version (CADP2) is shown at D. Here, we see much greater coverage detail in which various crosshatch patterns are used to identify specific sound pressure levels on the seating plane.

The program and engineering sub-routines were written by James Day, D. B. Keele, and David Albertz.

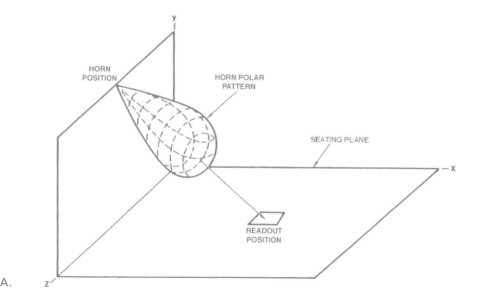

A. Basic principle of CADP.

B. CADP coverage on seating planes.

C. Views of loudspeaker array.

D. High resolution coverage via CADP2.

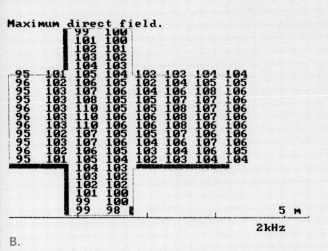

Maximum direct field.

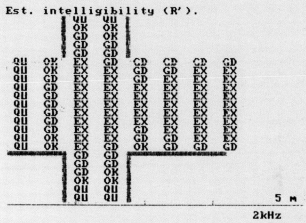

Est. intelligibility (R').

B.

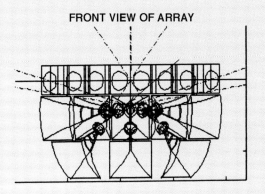

FRONT VIEW OF ARRAY

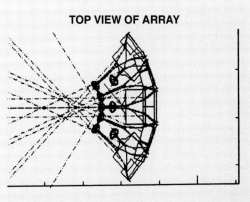

TOP VIEW OF ARRAY

C.

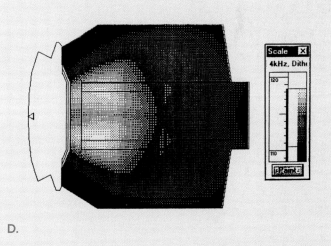

D.

Rapid-Flare Horns and Drivers

Historically, compression drivers were used as low as 400 and 500 Hz in early motion picture and monitoring systems. For these systems to load properly, both driver and horn must have a fairly slow flare rate. The price paid for the slow flare rate is an increase in second harmonic distortion at high operating levels, and this has been an inevitable consequence of horn systems from their inception. In recent years the industry has migrated to heavy-duty cone systems, both horn and non-horn loaded, for midrange applications, and it is no longer necessary for high frequency compression drivers to have slow flare rates.

In the early 1990s, JBL introduced a new series of Rapid-Flare drivers and horns, all of which were intended for use above 800 to 1000 Hz. The motor structures of these new drivers are the same as before, but the initial flare rate is much more rapid, as shown at A and B.

The response of the standard driver/horn configuration is shown at C. (These curves were run with the fundamental signal maintained at 108 dB SPL at a distance of 1 meter from the mouth of the horn.) The distortion curve has been raised 20 dB for convenience in reading. Similar curves are shown at D for the new driver mounted on a new horn of equivalent size and coverage characteristics. The improvement in distortion is quite clear in the range from 2 kHz to 8 kHz.

A. Details of traditional design.

B. Details of newer design.

C. Second harmonic distortion, traditional design.

D. Second harmonic distortion, newer design.

NEW DRIVER CONFIGURATION

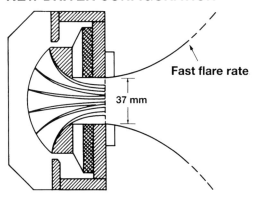

Fast flare rate

37 mm

B.

NEW DRIVER/HORN COMBINATION

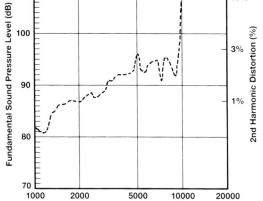

D.

STANDARD DRIVER CONFIGURATION

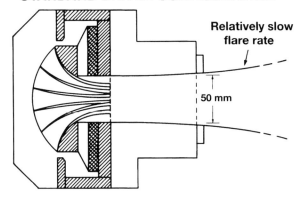

Relatively slow
flare rate

50 mm

A.

STANDARD DRIVER/HORN COMBINATION

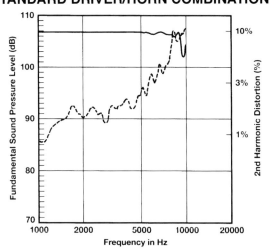

C.

Vented Gap Cooling(VGC) of JBL's Low-Frequency Drivers

JBL's low frequency transducers are widely used in high-level music reinforcement applications where they are stressed very close to their thermal limits. Over the years the company has made significant development in adhesives, heat-resistant materials, and construction techniques that minimize the effects of excessive heating. Long before a driver fails because of voice coil burnout, its performance suffers in several regards. The heating of a voice coil results in an increase in its resistance, and this reduces the sensitivity of the transducer. The resistance increase also causes a noticeable change in the balance between very low frequencies and the midband.

In a typical closed magnetic motor structure, heat from the voice coil is transmitted to the structural elements primarily by radiation and air conduction, and the resulting rise in temperature conveys the heat to the outer structure of the transducer. The large effective area of the outer structure further dissipates heat via radiation and convection.

JBL's Vented Gap Cooling (VGC) was developed by engineer Douglas Button, and it provides a means of introducing convection cooling earlier in the overall heat removal cycle. A rear view of the motor structure of a typical low frequency transducer is shown at A, and three openings are clearly visible. These openings extend all the way to the voice coil/magnetic gap region of the motor and provide a "pumping" action that removes heated air from the interior of the motor. In addition, the arraying of these openings around the periphery of the structure provides an added air convection path, which air enters via the lower opening and exits at the upper openings. The net result of these actions is an improvement in the steadystate "safe temperature" power rating of the transducer. The design is covered by U. S. Patent 5,042,072.

A section view of the transducer is shown at B with the air pumping action indicated. A photo showing perspective views of two VGC drivers is shown at C.

A. Back view of magnetic structure.

B. Section view of driver.

C. Photos of typical vented gap drivers.

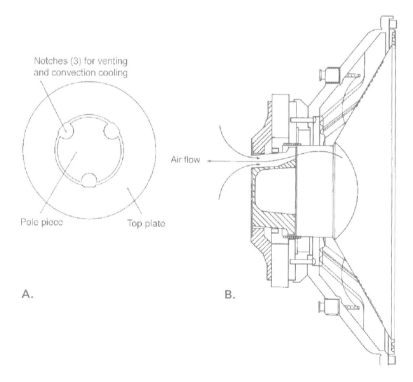

Notches (3) for venting
and convection cooling

Air flow

Pole piece   Top plate

A.   B.

Air flow

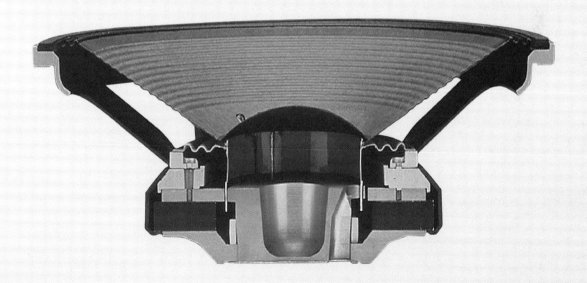

C.

JBL's Differential Drive® Magnetic Structures

By the end of the 20th century, neodymium based magnetic materials had become an economical reality in routine loudspeaker design. This rare earth element was the main constituent in what are referred to as NIB magnets, a combination of neodymium, iron, and boron. This material has a very high magnetic coercive force and can be used in relatively small quantities to produce high magnetic flux densities in standard loudspeaker motor structures made of iron materials. A minimum of iron is required, and the form factor of these new structures can result in new solutions to traditional design problems.

Over the years, JBL's 4-inch diameter voice coils represented the best solution to high dynamic force requirements in cone transducer design. Taking advantage of NIB's very high coercive force, it was now possible to design a new motor structure that employed two active magnetic gaps in series, with sufficient flux density in each gap to attain the necessary mechanical force to control the loud-speaker's moving system. The new design was smaller in diameter, but had greater front-back mechanical depth. Because much less iron was required in the magnetic circuit, the overall weight of the motor was significantly less than in earlier designs. The remaining problems were principally those of adequate heat removal from the smaller magnetic structure.

From JBL's marketing point of view, the prospect of lighter-weight drivers was especially attractive in the area of line arrays, which usually require large numbers of systems suspended from a single overhead point. There were also attractive prospects for weight and cost reduction in consumer systems intended for music-on-the-go.

Under the Differential Drive mark, JBL has introduced a large range of new transducer designs that take advantage of NIB magnets. A simple technical comparison between the traditional approach and the new approach is shown at A. The single coil in the traditional structure provides all of the motive force. In the Differential Drive version, two smaller coils are used, working in series, to provide an equivalent net force on the moving system.

A detailed cutaway view of a typical Differential Drive transducer is shown at B, and a photograph of a typical Differential Drive low frequency transducer is shown at C.

The design is covered by U. S. Patent 5,748,760 and other foreign patents. Additional patents have been issued covering variations on the placement of the voice coils and shorting rings to optimize linearity and minimize distortion.

A. Section views of traditional and Differential Drive magnetic structures.

B. Cutaway view of a Differential Drive structure.

C. Photo of Differential Drive transducer.

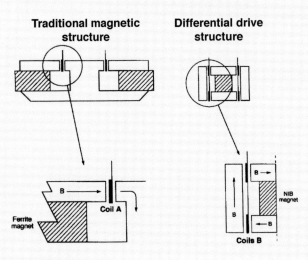

Traditional magnetic structure

B

Coil A

Ferrite magnet

Differential drive structure

B

B

B

NIB magnet

Coils B

A.

C.

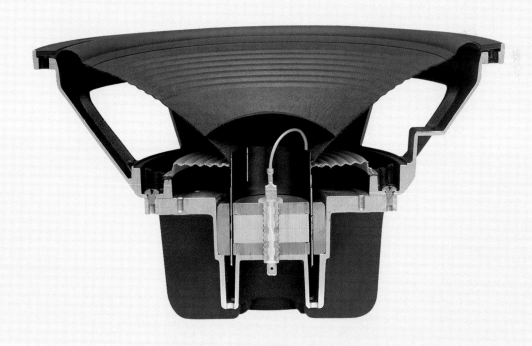

B.

Spin-o-rama Measurements on Loudspeaker Systems

Casually referred to as Spin-o-rama measurements, Floyd Toole and the acoustical research group of JBL's parent company, Harman International Industries, have devised an automated measurement technique that defines the complex nature of three-dimensional sound radiation from a loudspeaker system as it performs in a normal home-type environment. JBL, as well as other members of the corporate family, are able to take advantage of these refined techniques.

A typical anechoic (reflection-free) environment used in loudspeaker measurements is shown at A, and the spin-o-rama measurement setup is shown at B. A total of 70 wide-band measurements are made, and extensive "number-crunching" yields the curves shown at C. The labeled curves are defined as:

1. Direct sound
2. Normal listening window response
3. Early reflection contributions
4. Loudspeaker power response
5. Directivity index, based on early reflections
6. Directivity index, based on power response

The upper set of curves at C represents an excellent system, with uniform on-axis response and smooth families of off-axis data. The lower set of curves represents a system that could be termed "OK," but which has some remaining problems regarding off-axis uniformity to be solved.

A. Photo of anechoic chamber.

B. Positions of measurements.

C. Typical "Spin-o-rama" curves.

Systems that exhibit uniform on- and off-axis response routinely score higher on subjective listening tests than those systems with irregularities. This is true regardless of prior conditioning of listeners and their specific cultural backgrounds. The correlation is in fact remarkable, and the measurement technique is now considered a benchmark in subjective measurement of loudspeakers. All data courtesy of Alan Devantier and Floyd Toole.

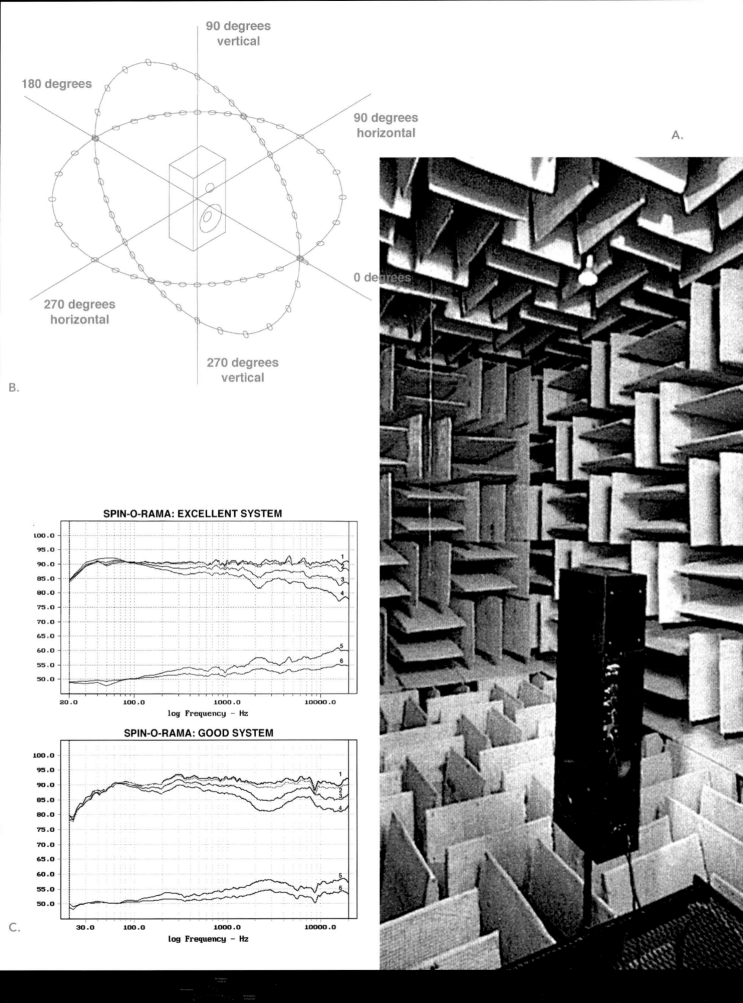

90 degrees
vertical

180 degrees

90 degrees
horizontal

0 degrees

270 degrees
horizontal

270 degrees
vertical

A.

B.

SPIN-O-RAMA: EXCELLENT SYSTEM

log Frequency – Hz

SPIN-O-RAMA: GOOD SYSTEM

log Frequency – Hz

C.

JBL's EON® Family of Portable Products

The immensely successful EON product line was introduced in 1995 and was aimed at small-scale music and speech reinforcement for people on the go. It consists of two full-range systems and a subwoofer. A small 8-by-2 mixer is also available, as are various mounting fixtures. The most remarkable aspect of the product group is the ultra-low weight of its high performance systems. The loudspeaker frames and horns are integral with the cast aluminum front baffles, providing excellent heat dissipation and relatively low mass. The loudspeaker drivers themselves are of the Differential Drive type, contributing as well to low mass. (The weight of the EON models is roughly 20 pounds lower than systems offering equivalent performance.) The built-in "smart" electronics ensure component protection under all operating conditions.

A group photo of EON products is shown at A. In addition to the powered models, there are also passive versions. A typical reinforcement application is shown at B, where the small mixer has added capability of plug-in effects and multiple program sources. Where utmost simplicity is desired, microphones can be plugged directly into the loudspeaker electronics, bypassing the mixer altogether.

The details shown at C gives an idea of the multiple design aspects of the front baffle, accommodating both high frequency horn and low frequency frame. The relatively thin baffle cross-section is reinforced by closely spaced ribs, further contributing to the light weight and strength of the system. The TTMS® (Total Thermal Management System®) has been issued U. S. Patent 5,533,132.

A.

15 in powered subwoofer

10 in 2-way biamped loudspeaker

15 in 2-way biamped loudspeaker

B.

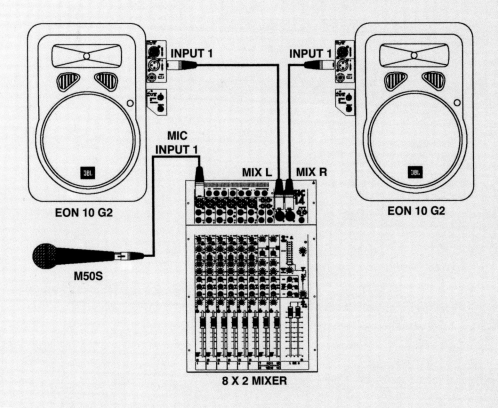

INPUT 1   INPUT 1

MIC
INPUT 1

MIX L   MIX R

EON 10 G2   EON 10 G2

M50S

8 X 2 MIXER

A. EON product group.

B. Signal flow diagram for typical EON application.

C. Front and rear baffle design details.

FRONT OF BAFFLE   REAR OF BAFFLE

C.

JBL's VerTec® Line Arrays

Line arrays have been studied and analyzed for more than three-quarters of a century, yet their contribution to sophisticated system design has been realized only in the last 20 or so years. Modern designs are far lighter than older ones, and this means that truly long arrays can be safely suspended in public places. Line arrays have played an important in JBL's design history, but the modern VerTec elements, along with their unique design methodology, now provide a substantial step forward in performance.

A typical large 12-element array is shown at A. At 159 pounds each, these elements are among the lighter ones in the industry. An array of 18 elements can be accommodated for controlled vertical coverage over distances in excess of 500 feet.

The line drawings shown at B give design details of the basic system. Crucial here is the vertical arraying of three high-frequency horn elements that are virtually contiguous, producing a "ribbon" sound source essential for proper response at high frequencies in the far field.

An essential element in the VerTec concept is a system design program that allows users to observe estimated directional response while the job is still on the drawing board. Two aspects of this program are shown at C. At the left is a physical view of the array showing the articulation of loudspeaker elements. At the right is a set of polar response curves showing the system's response in the vertical plane. Here, you can clearly see the increase in the system's coverage at large distances, which is due to the straight, upper portion of the line array. Theory and development of the JBL Line Array Calculator software design program were carried out by Mark Ureda.

A. Photo of a 12-element array.

B. Three views of basic array element.

C. Displays of array side view and vertical polar response.

A.

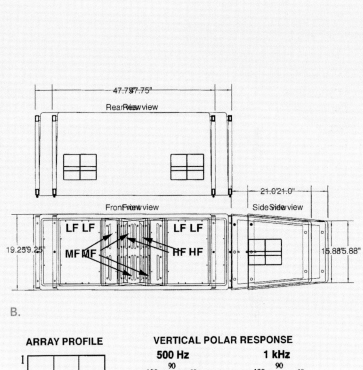

Rear View view

47.75" 47.75"

Front View view   Side Side view

21.0' 21.0"

19.25' 9.25"   LF LF   LF LF

MF MF   HF HF

15.88' 5.88"

B.

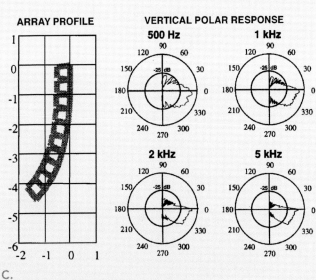

ARRAY PROFILE

VERTICAL POLAR RESPONSE

500 Hz   1 kHz

2 kHz   5 kHz

C.

Precision Directivity™ (PD) Pattern Control

A.

For many indoor sports arenas, especially where there may be high spectator noise, it is essential to have high directivity at both low and high frequencies in order to maintain adequate intelligibility. At mid (MF) and high frequencies (HF) uniform directivity can be attained over a wide range by mounting the HF horn in the mouth of the MF horn. Through careful adjustment of both spatial relationships, along with appropriate delay and equalization, two radiating systems, as shown at **A**, will exhibit uniform directivity in their crossover zone, as shown at **B**.

Below about 250 Hz, each element in an array of low frequency drivers can be individually driven to produce excellent directivity, along with high output capability.

The technique of "end firing" a line array to increase its on-axis directivity is well known and is described here. Front and side views of a 20-element array are shown at **C**. The firing pattern is shown at **D**. Here, the launch angle of sound is tilted 35 degrees downward as the various elements are sequentially driven relative to the reference loudspeaker, which has a delay of zero. The net result of the sequential firing is a coherent wave, so to speak, aimed 35 degrees downward, as shown at **D**. The directivity index is in the range of 9 to 12 dB for frequencies in the range from 160 to 250 Hz, as shown at **E**. Each transducer firing zone of course requires its own amplifier and delay function.

A. View of a mid-high-frequency PD model covering the range above 250 Hz.

B. Combined directivity of mid and high elements.

C. Side and front views of low frequency PD array.

D. Side view of array showing firing pattern.

E. Directional properties of low frequency PD array.

D.

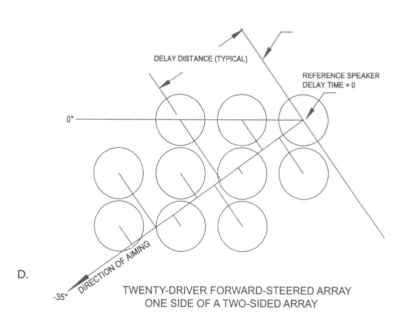

DELAY DISTANCE (TYPICAL)

REFERENCE SPEAKER
DELAY TIME = 0

0°

DIRECTION OF AIMING

-35°

TWENTY-DRIVER FORWARD-STEERED ARRAY
ONE SIDE OF A TWO-SIDED ARRAY

Horizontal Beamwidth (-6 dB)

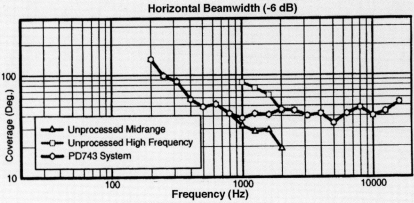

B.

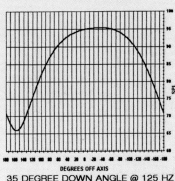

35 DEGREE DOWN ANGLE @ 125 HZ

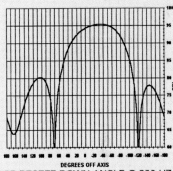

35 DEGREE DOWN ANGLE @ 200 HZ

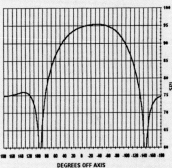

35 DEGREE DOWN ANGLE @ 160 HZ

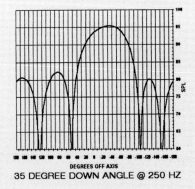

35 DEGREE DOWN ANGLE @ 250 HZ

UPPER TRUSS MODULE

PD162L4   PD162   PD162   PD162U4

LOWER TRUSS MODULE

SIDE VIEW

FRONT VIEW

C.

E.

One-inch Beryllium Ultra-High-Frequency Driver

The success of high-density digital recording has brought with it the need for loudspeaker high-frequency transducers whose response reaches out to 50 kHz. JBL's 045 Be compression driver is shown in cross-section at **A**, and its frequency response, mounted on a plane wave tube, is as shown at **B**. In application, this driver is mounted on a very small horn with a 0.35-inch diameter throat. Horizontal and vertical –6-dB beamwidth plots are shown at **C**. A photo of the horn-driver is shown at **D**.

The element beryllium exhibits very high stiffness and light weight, both of which are essential characteristics in attaining extended ultra-high-frequency response. When we consider that the wavelength of sound at 50 kHz is in the range of 0.25 inch, we can appreciate the degree of precision and consistency required in the construction of such a driver. The phasing plug itself is manufactured as a single structure via a technique known as stereo lithography, a method for actually "growing" a mechanical element as opposed to assembling it. Likewise, the forming of the beryllium dome and spacing relative to the phasing plug are critical. Tim Prenta, of the JBL Consumer Engineering staff, designed the 045 Be compression driver. Other beryllium drivers in the company's transducer lineup include models with both 3-inch and 4-inch diaphragms.

A. Section view of 045Be compression driver.

B. 045Be driver response on a plane wave tube.

C. Beamwidth of 035Be driver mounted on 0.35-inch throat horn.

D. Photo of 035Be driver with horn.

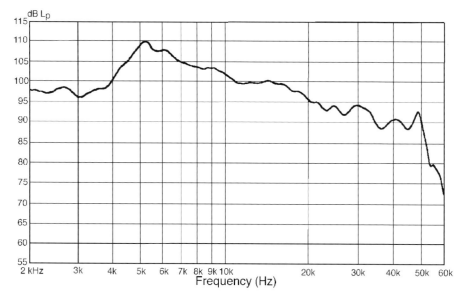

B.

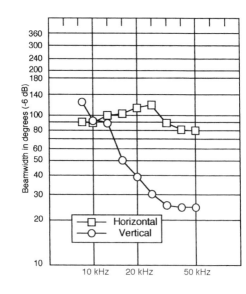

C.

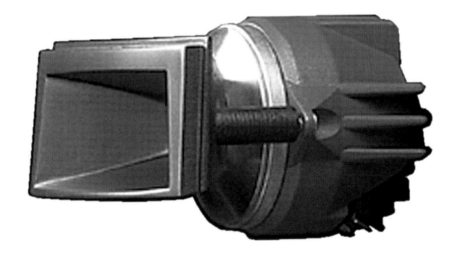

D.

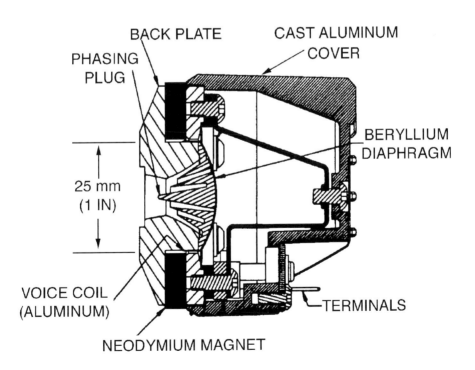

BACK PLATE CAST ALUMINUM
COVER

PHASING
PLUG

25 mm
(1 IN)

BERYLLIUM
DIAPHRAGM

VOICE COIL
(ALUMINUM)

TERMINALS

NEODYMIUM MAGNET

A.

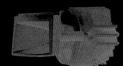

JBL's ScreenArray® Systems for Cinema Applications

As digital recording made great strides in both production sound acquisition and in field exhibition, during the mid 1990s JBL revisited its priorities in the areas of cinema sound coverage, distortion, and in the form factor of screen channel systems. Typical here is the 4632 ScreenArray system shown at **A**. While the system stands fairly high, the depth is only 17.75 inches, a fact much appreciated by theater owners.

Performance considerations included:

> 1. Uniformity of vertical and horizontal coverage angles over as wide a range as practicable.
> 2. A nominal 10-degree downward tilt in the launch angle at mid and high frequencies for more uniform coverage in modern cinemas.
> 3. Use of JBL's developments in the areas of rapid-flare horns and drivers to minimize distortion.

These goals were substantially met through the application of array theory, development of a new family of cone drivers suitable for use on horns and waveguides, and the implementation of advanced dividing network design.

Performance characteristics of the 4632 system are shown at **B**. The upper curve shows the uniformity of on-axis response in the cinema. The lower set of curves shows the remarkable uniformity of pattern control in vertical and horizontal planes.

The designers of these systems were JBL engineers Bernard Werner and William Gelow.

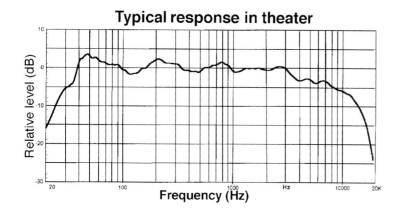

Typical response in theater

A. Photo of JBL 4632 ScreenArray system.

B. On-axis and beamwidth response of JBL 4632 ScreenArray system. Narrowing of horizontal coverage angle compensates for cinema screen high frequency spreading.

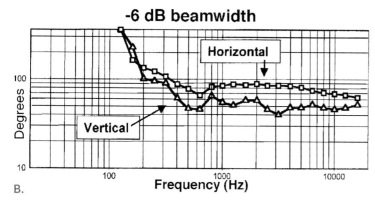

-6 dB beamwidth

B.

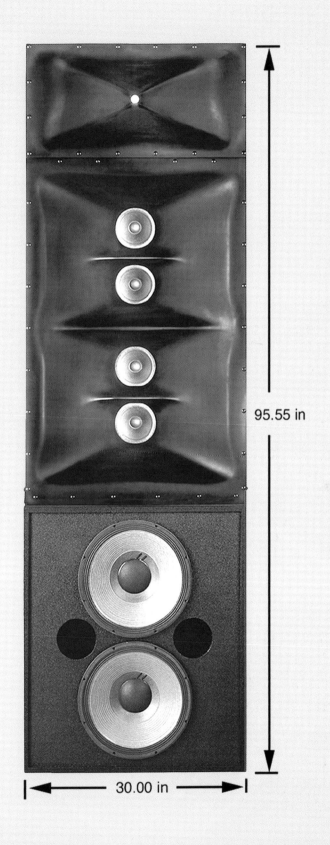

95.55 in

30.00 in

A.

Chapter 3: Corporate Identification and Graphic Standards
Introduction

Little time or money was available in the early days of LMC to donate to corporate identification or the design of a company logo. In the late 1920s one could scarcely identify a professional graphics designer to take on such a project, and in many cases the design of a company's identifying mark was an informal collaboration between the company president and the local print shop. In this chapter we will review the broad array of designs, both for print media and for product identification, that have been used over three-quarters of a century by LMC and JBL.

Lansing Manufacturing Company

Graphic Standards: During its first years the Lansing Manufacturing Company (LMC) made small, low-cost loudspeakers for radio set manufacturers. The company basically had no need for a defining trademark, and the simple banner shown at Figure **1A** was sufficient. In the early 1930s, LMC developed a technical association with the sound department of MGM Studios in the design and production of the so-called Shearer cinema sound loudspeaker. With this move, the company and its principals were clearly progressing professionally, and perhaps the prestige of the Hollywood/MGM association called for more formal graphic standards. The earlier letterhead from the late twenties thus gave way to more elegant ones reflecting the prevailing art deco influences of the day, as shown at Figure **1B** and **C**.

The heading of a product bulletin introducing the mid-1930s LMC Iconic monitor system is shown at Figure **1D**. The quasi-script "Lansing" used here had actually dated back to LMC's earliest days, and was to become a central element in the company's later graphics design.

Product Identification: LMC products of the late 1920s were primarily loudspeaker units for use in radio sets. There was little need for anything more than a stock or model number, often a water-transfer decal, to be placed on the device. Figure **2** (see page 102) shows a view of such a decal on the back of an early LMC radio-type loudspeaker. This unit is the earliest product in JBL's historical collection, and it is estimated to have been built in the late 1920s or early 1930s.

Professional models developed for MGM and other cinema projects carried a more durable metallic "boiler plate" label affixed to the product, as shown at Figure **3A** (see page 102). A rendering of such a label is shown at **3B**.

A. LANSING MANUFACTURING CO.

LOS ANGELES ❦ CALIFORNIA

Printed in U.S.A.—Pridemark

B. **LANSING MFG. CO.**

6626 McKinley St.   Los Angeles, Calif.

C. **Lansing** MANUFACTURING CO.

6900 McKinley Ave. «» Los Angeles, Calif.

D. BULLETIN No. 4

ICONIC

LOUD SPEAKER SYSTEMS

Figure 1.   Early LMC printed graphics

Figure 2.   Photo of LMC decal on back cover of early product.

A.   B.

Figure 3.   Graphic identification of LMC professional products.

James B. Lansing Sound, Incorporated

When his contract with Altec Lansing expired in 1946, Lansing was ready once again to strike out on his own, forming Lansing Sound, Incorporated. Figure 4 shows the new company mark as it appeared at the bottom of a product bulletin for a the D 101 15-inch loudspeaker. This bulletin described the first product of the new company and is assumed to be among the earliest publications of the company.

Altec Lansing management took immediate issue with the name of Lansing's new company, stating that it would cause confusion in the marketplace. They also took issue with the use of the trademark ICONIC that appeared in the same publication. Matters were settled out of court, and the name of the new company was subsequently changed to James B. Lansing Sound, Incorporated.

Altec Lansing agreed with this change, inasmuch as the new name emphasized the man himself and not the previous company. Lansing also initiated the use of his personal signature and his informal name "Jim"—in print as well as on certain products—as a further means of identifying himself and his products.

Graphic Standards: At the time, there was no logo per se, and a number of marks were used by James B. Lansing Sound from 1947 to about 1955. Some of these are shown in Figure 5 (see page 104):

A. Jim Lansing stylized signature, both normal and reversed.

B. Jim Lansing Signature, with large script "L".

C. James B. Lansing, with large script "L".

Figure 6 on page 104 shows usage in advertising with the full company name (A) and the informal Jim Lansing (B).

Figure 7A on page 105 shows the paper label that was used on the magnet structure of early D130 production at San Marcos. At B we show the typical use of the "Signature" water decal on later D130 production.

Figure 4.   Earliest print graphics of Lansing Sound Incorporated.

A.

B.

C.

Figure 5.   Early JBL "Signature" logos in print form

A.

B.

Figure 6.   Examples of JBL identification in single-column ads in the early 1950s. The significance of the highlighted "La" is not known. It may have been a reference to Los Angeles.

A.

B.

Figure 7.   Examples of "Signature" decals on D130 and D131 drivers (circa 1947 and 1953).

By the mid 1950s, William Thomas, saw the need for a distinguishing logo to give focus to the company's steadily rising fortunes. There was a special need for this in foreign markets, where a clear logo was taken as a sign of company stability. He secured the services of noted West Coast graphics designer Jerome Gould, whose basic conception was that of a triangle placed atop a circle containing the letters JBL. There was no single form of the new logo, and a great deal of freedom was exercised in its application over the period of about a decade. One may think of it more as a design template than a logo per se.

The basic print form of the logo is shown at Figure 8. Other print versions included a solid form with no letters visible and a reverse version placed in a rectangle. Variations are shown at Figure 9A (normal, without letters) and B (reversed, without letters).

Other variations of the logo are shown at Figure 10: a mixture of old and new motifs is shown at A; B shows the use of the logo as notes on a musical staff. The view at C shows a logo containing product photographs, and at D only the circular portion of the logo is used.

Two whimsical uses are shown at Figure 11 (see page 108): the logos as ordinal numbers (A); the logo morphing into a Christmas tree (B).

Figure 8.   Basic Gould logo in print form.

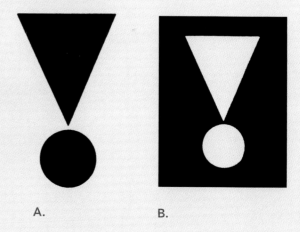

A.   B.

Figure 9.   Normal and reversed logos without letters.

A.

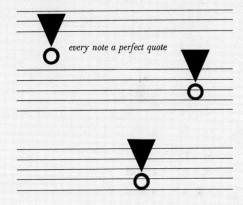

every note a perfect quote

B.

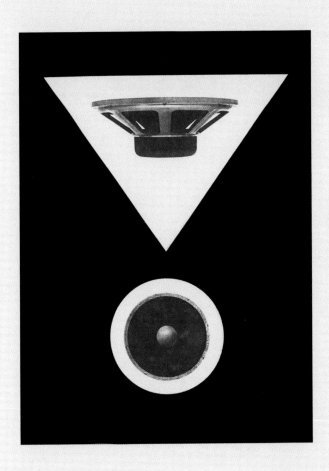

C.

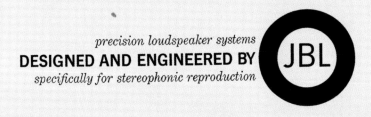

precision loudspeaker systems
DESIGNED AND ENGINEERED BY JBL
specifically for stereophonic reproduction

D.

Figure 10.   Other logo variations.

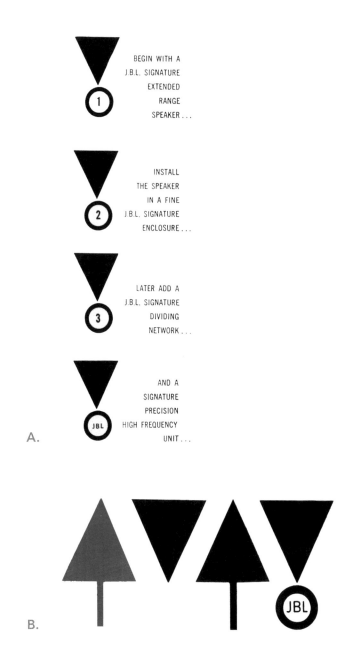

A.

BEGIN WITH A
J.B.L. SIGNATURE
EXTENDED
RANGE
SPEAKER...

INSTALL
THE SPEAKER
IN A FINE
J.B.L. SIGNATURE
ENCLOSURE...

LATER ADD A
J.B.L. SIGNATURE
DIVIDING
NETWORK...

AND A
SIGNATURE
PRECISION
HIGH FREQUENCY
UNIT...

B.

Figure 11.   "Deconstruction" of the logo.

Company Letterhead: Figure 12 shows the company letterhead used from about 1955 to 1965. The triangle in the Gould logo has been narrowed somewhat, perhaps to be in better agreement with the small and lean lettering above it.

Product Identification: For identification of loudspeaker systems, a family of attractive die-cast emblems (or "badges") was created, and reconstructions of four of these are shown at Figure 13 on page 110. These were affixed to the front grilles of loudspeaker systems and could be clearly discerned across a large living room. They conveyed a sense of value as only a three-dimensional piece of metal can. The version shown at A has a clear relief between the symbol and background, and the raised portion has been brushed. In the versions shown at B the relief has been filled with matte black plastic prior to brushing so that there is only a single layer. The complex version shown at C was used on the grilles or front surfaces of large systems such as the Hartsfield. It was difficult to make, and the side extensions were easily broken.

For identification of consumer electronics products a similar set of thin metal emblems were attached to the front panels as shown in Figure 14 on page 110. Individual transducers and components were labeled with metal "foilcals" and cast metal details, as shown at Figures 15A and B on page 111.

JAMES B. LANSING SOUND, INC. *3249 casitas ave. · los angeles, calif. 90039 · telephone 665-4101*

Figure 12.   JBL company letterhead from about 1955 to 1965.

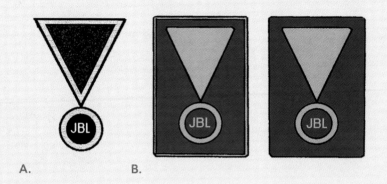

A.   B.

C.

Figure 13.   Die-cast logos for use on grilles of loudspeaker systems.

Figure 14.   Use of logos on consumer electronics products.

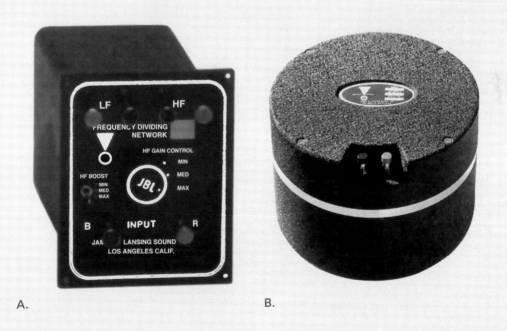

A.   B.

Figure 15.   Use of logos on dividing networks and transducer products.

During the mid 1960s, William Thomas and his marketing staff had come to the conclusion that the Gould logo, original and inspired as it was, had lost much its original corporate value. It had been used, and abused, in many ways, and the clash of associated type fonts often made it the plaything of advertising people. Arnold Wolf, whose prior association with the company had been in innovative industrial design, was chosen to develop a new logo—the one we know today. Along with the basic design, Wolf provided a usage manual that clearly indicates how the logo should, and should not, be applied. Such matters as size, layout, association with related marks and the like, are all covered in great detail. The primary directive is that proportions within the logo are not to be changed or altered in any way, and that only the approved versions in the usage manual are to be directly and literally copied for all applications. Under no condition is the logo to be redrawn for any purpose. These rules still prevail in the company today. Wolf retained the exclamation point, reducing its size proportionally and placing it over the crook in the "J."The "JBL" lettering is unique, and the whole is placed in a bold rectangle.

The logo is one of the most highly recognized and respected marks in the audio industry worldwide. Although it is now more than 40 years old, it seems timeless and is as fresh today as it was in 1965. The basic print form of the logo is shown at Figure 16A, and the traditional background color is medium red-orange, rigorously defined graphically as Pantone PMS 172. (An alternate color is the greenish-grey PMS 403.) Other versions, with and without backgrounds, are shown at B and C. The version shown at D was designed for print use by the JBL Professional division of Harman International Industries when that company was formed in the mid 1980s.

Figure 16.   Details of the Wolf logo design.

Company Letterhead: The present JBL Professional letterhead is shown at Figure 17. The narrow gray rectangle surrounding the basic logo represents that portion of the bond paper that has been embossed by a hot stamp before printing. The effect is one of subtle bas relief as the page is normally viewed.

Product Identification: The logo version shown earlier at Figure 16E is used as a template for metal die casting in which the border and letters are raised over a recessed background, as indicated. Subtle dimensional changes have been made here to compensate for possible distortions due to draft angles and to facilitate the actual molding process itself. This form is used primarily for product identification, and the raised portion, if metal is used, is normally "brushed" for clarity of detail.

Figure 18A (see page 114) shows a family of both die cast and plastic molded logos intended for front mounting on specific loudspeaker systems. The larger molded item is in bold "JBL orange" and can be clearly identified as such when mounted on systems used for sound reinforcement in large public spaces. Figure 18B shows a unique form of the logo in which the letters are back-lit via light-emitting diodes. This design is used on the front baffle of a powered loudspeaker system.

Figure 19 (see page 115) shows the use of both foilcals and integral die casting of the logo in the identification of individual components.

Figure 20 (see page 115) shows an innovative form of the logo. Here, the logo details are delineated in stencil fashion on a heavy metal screen which acts as a protective grille on a professional sound reinforcement loudspeaker system. These systems are normally arrayed vertically, often as many as twelve to eighteen in a set. The repeating JBL logos make a statement for the company that is both subtle and powerful by way of repetition.

JBL Professional, P.O. Box 2200, 8500 Balboa Boulevard, Northridge, CA 91329

JBL

Figure 17.   Current JBL Professional letterhead.

A.

B.

Figure 18.   A family of die-cast and plastic molded logos (A); an "electronic" logo. On the front of a powered loudspeaker system, the lettering of this logo lights up when the system is on (B.).

Figure 19.   Logos in the form of foilcals and integral casting on transducer components.

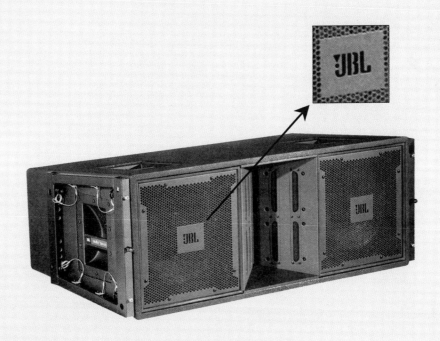

Figure 20.   Here, logos are a part of the perforated metal grille design.

Chapter 4: Consumer Products

From the company's inception in 1946, the consumer marketplace has been a major driving force in product development. The professional market as we know it today was far in the future, but the consumer market was here and now. The rise of home high fidelity, which owed much to developments in England, was shaping a new concern for quality loudspeakers. Such companies as Tannoy and Wharfdale led this move, along with a host of US companies centered basically in the Northeast and on the West Coast.

The earliest JBL loudspeakers were intended for retrofitting into high-end phonograph consoles, and with the advent of the Long Playing record, this interest expanded quickly. In the early 1950s, JBL's introduction of the Hartsfield system signified a first for the industry – a "statement" loudspeaker that took its place as a major piece of furniture in the modern living room as well as a reproducer of sound. Its only competitor was Paul Klipsch's Klipschorn.

The introduction of stereophonic sound in the late 1950s in effect doubled the loudspeaker requirement, and such models as the Hartsfield were ultimately destined to go away. JBL's Paragon, introduced at the beginning of the stereo era, showed how a single large enclosure could satisfy the demands of stereo reproduction, and its 25-year existence in the company's catalog underscores its success. For JBL, large furniture pieces became dominant, eventually yielding to the demand for smaller floor-standing models and so-called bookshelf systems.

A major development for JBL was the identification of recording monitor systems with corresponding home models during the early 1970s. The Century L100 was a product of this era, and it set new sales records for the industry.

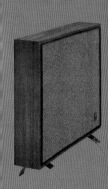

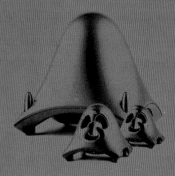

As recording technology developed, more attention was paid to refining basic loudspeaker response. New measurement technology came on the scene, and all loudspeaker manufacturers began to pay more attention to basic performance criteria, such as on-axis response uniformity, overall pattern control, left-right baffle symmetry, and time-domain behavior. This last parameter was new to the "performance list" and was eventually to become very significant as digital recording entered and ultimately dominated the scene.

By the mid-1980s, automotive stereo was becoming a more important aspect of consumer loudspeaker marketing. It was soon followed by attention to sound-for-video, as matrixed stereo provided the rudiments of surround sound. Finally, with the development of the DVD, the home audio system has morphed into a larger digitally controlled entertainment center extending beyond audio and video, well into the domain of personal computers and peripheral devices.

Through its 60 years, JBL has relied on the talents of relatively few industrial and graphic designers. Alvin Lustig, Roger Kennedy, and Jerome Gould were on hand during the early years, followed by Arnold Wolf and Doug Warner. In later years Dan Ashcraft has been a major player in the industrial design of consumer products.

In this chapter we will document the development of JBL consumer products through early product specification sheets, ads, and detailed product photographs.

This is the cover page of a rare catalog from JBL's early factory location in Venice, CA. The date is 1947 or 1948.

JBL's 1950 Two-Page Catalog

In 1950, JBL's catalog consisted of four loudspeaker components, two enclosure types, and one dividing network. Each enclosure was available in one of three finishes so that the total number of options for the user was fairly broad. The cone drivers were: D130 (15"), D131 (12"), and D208 (8"), and each enclosure could accommodate each of the cone drivers. The tradition of mixing and matching components was established early in the high fidelity era and underscored the role of consumer as avid hobbyist.

The Hartsfield (1954)

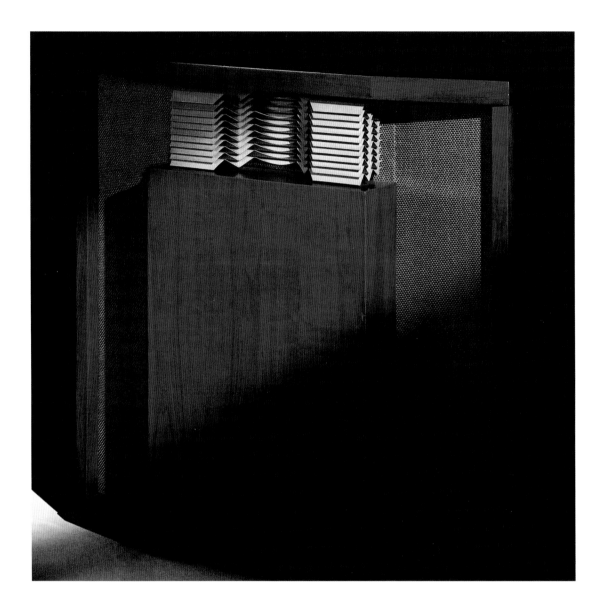

Based on a low frequency corner horn designed by William Hartsfield, this three-way, all-horn system won praise from audio critics and the general press. It was intended for corner placement and was considered the apex of loudspeaker technology of its day. The system is still made by a few independent builders both in the United States and in Japan. (Photo courtesy Stereo Sound)

JBL Enclosures, 1956 Catalog

C34

Rear-loaded Corner Console Horn

The C34 contains a 6' exponential folded horn that delivers an extra octave of clean, crisp bass. Corner placement is not required. From 150 cps, on down, energy from the back of a 15" speaker radiates through the horn. Above 150 cps, the speaker acts as a direct radiator.

C35 C37

Console Reflex

Here are superbly engineered enclosures for JBL *Signature Sound* Systems that are precision made and assembled without compromise.

C35

C37

C36 /C38

Console Reflex

Here in minimum volume is a reflex enclosure engineered to deliver full range response when used with JBL extended range speakers.

C36

C38

C550

Rearloaded Folded Horn

Designed originally for theaters, the 550 has a folded exponential horn path 8' long. The horn is coupled to the rear surface of two 15" low frequency units. Above the acoustical crossover point of 175 cps, the speakers act as direct radiators. Not available in birch wood.

C31

Frontloaded Corner Horn

Two fifteen-inch low frequency drivers with large combined piston area, plus precise exponential curves built into the formed dual horn are responsible for extended low end. Energy from the back side of both speakers is fed into carefully designed reflex chambers for additional low end loading.

C435

Rearloaded Folded Horn

Designed for small theaters, the C435 is similar to the C550 but will house only one low frequency driver with a consequent reduction in cabinet width. The slow taper rate and long horn path result in exceptional bass fundamentals. Furnished in rough theater black only.

By the mid-1950s, the mix-and-match concept was in full swing, offering the JBL buyer even more options. In addition to reflex (ported) enclosures, a variety of horn loaded designs had been adapted from the cinema activities the company was supporting. The back-loaded horns eventually found their way into the professional area, and were popular with early specialists in high-level music reinforcement. Note in the two lower right panels that the small format perforated plate acoustic lens had replaced the earlier small multicellular horn.

Selecting JBL Components in the 1950s and 1960s

A typical JBL enclosure and design chart are shown here. The buyer selects an enclosure from the left column and checks the various driver combinations that will fit that enclosure. The component combinations are shown across the top of the chart.

For example, the C34 back-loaded horn enclosure shown here can accommodate two transducer combinations, 001 and 030. The 001 combination includes a 15-inch low frequency driver with a horn/lens combination. The second combination, 030, uses the full-range 15-inch D130 driver, topped off by the 075 UHF unit for extended high frequencies. Ordering systems such as these demanded a knowledgeable dealer and a patient buyer.

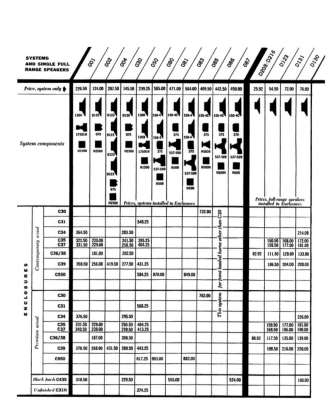

The Paragon Group

The 1957 Paragon was based on a direct-reflecting design by Richard Ranger originally intended for application in motion picture stereophonic reproduction. A mid-size version, the Metregon, was introduced later, as was a smaller bookshelf design, the Minigon. The curved cylindrical section balanced direct and reflected signals to produce a broad stereo sound stage for listeners over a fairly wide listening angle. Arnold Wolf was the industrial designer of the original Paragon. (Photo courtesy Stereo Sound)

Paragon

Metregon

Minigon models

JBL T-Circuit Electronics

JBL's "T-Circuit" electronics made use of a unique output configuration designed by engineer Bart Locanthi and included the models shown here. At the top is the integrated preamp-amplifier (SA600); in the center is the SG520 Graphic Controller, and the SE400S solid state energizer is shown at the bottom of the figure. Other models in the electronics line included an amplifier unit intended for mounting in the rear of loudspeaker enclosures to provide direct powering for the system. These systems with "energizers" were the first of their kind in the high fidelity and professional markets. Arnold Wolf was the industrial designer for these electronics products. (Photo courtesy Stereo Sound)

The Olympus and Sovereign Systems

The Olympus and Sovereign shared the same components and enclosure dimensions. The elaborate fretwork grills set the Olympus apart, and that same motif was also used in the smaller Apollo system. Systems such as these typify the 1960s goal of high fidelity loudspeaker systems as fine furniture. (Photo courtesy Stereo Sound)

From the 1967 Catalog

The 1960s, first full decade of stereo, saw the influence of lean Northern European design trends on American products. It was also a time of artful black and white catalog photography, as shown here. The Viscount and Rhodes (center left and right) were the products of industrial designer Alvin Lustig.

The Trimline, lower left, met a need of the day for very shallow enclosures to more easily accommodate the requirements of stereo.

JBL in the mid-1960s was still perceived as a California company with a strong attachment to local designers and regional trends. The loudspeaker out-of-doors was scarcely given a thought elsewhere, but in Southern California it was a significant market.

Systems from the Early 1970s

Clockwise from upper left: Flair, Lancer 101, Lancer 77, Minuet, and Lancer 44. These systems, both floor-standing and bookshelf, represented the height of the "grille as artwork" era.

JBL Consumer Systems, 1971

A - Paragon
B - Flair L 45
C - Sovereign
D - Olympus
E - Lancer 55
F - L200
G - Aquarius
    Group
H - Verona
I - Century
J - Lancer 44
K - Cortina 88
L - Nova 88
M - Lancer
N - Athena
O - Minuet L75

The Aquarius Products

Designed in the latter half of the 1960s, the Aquarius products all made use of some degree of indirect sound radiation into the listening space. All of these models were executed in bold shapes and colors that were unusual in conventional design, but were well within JBL's established criteria. Of these models, the simple and slender Aquarius 4 was the most successful.

The Century L100

The Century L100 consumer system and the professional 4310/4311 models were acoustically identical. The L100 was available in a number of grille colors with an oiled walnut enclosure finish. The reticulated foam grille became a famous JBL statement in the early 1970s and spawned many imitators. During its lifetime the L100 became JBL's best selling bookshelf system and set industry records as well. A typical studio scene shows the 4311 in use on the meter bridge of a console, and the group shot, front to back, shows the models 4311, L100A, L100, and 4310.

L25 Prima Group

The Prima group consisted of a 2-way loudspeaker system, an equipment storage cabinet, and an equipment shelf. The enclosures were molded using a new material called "Acoustifoam." The upper and lower sides of the enclosures consisted of stepped sections that interlocked, making it easy and safe to stack the components in tight living spaces. The line was introduced in response to trends in lifestyle and home decor of the early 70s.

The Decade Series, Mid-1970s

The Decade products, ranging from a 2-way 8-inch to a 3-way 10-inch, positioned JBL as a player in the mid-price loudspeaker range at a time when large, furniture-type systems were on the wane. These models used wood veneer at a time when most of the industry had made the move to vinyl-clad particle board enclosures. The cone drivers in these systems had die-cast frames at a time when most of the industry was using stamped frames.

Big Monitors in the Home
Models L200 and L300

When the L100 "monitor in the home" was having its great success during the 1970s, JBL introduced the L200 (Studio Master) as a home version of the larger monitor format 4320 and the L300 (Summit) as a home version of the 3-way 4333. Since these models were floor-standing, their baffles were tilted back slightly to give an "upward launch" to the radiation pattern facing the intended listening position.

The L200 had a foam grille which echoed slightly that of the L100. The L300 made use of a stretch cloth grille and a reflective glass top. An "L400" was talked about for years, but it never materialized.

The Jubal and the Horizon

The Jubal L65 and Horizon L166 were notable systems from the 1975 - 1985 period. The floor-standing Jubal was the first "non-monitor" system in many years to make use of the slot-type 077 UHF ring radiator. The inset drawing, done in the style of Leonardo, is an echo of the JBL advertising style of the 1950s promoted by then-president Bill Thomas.

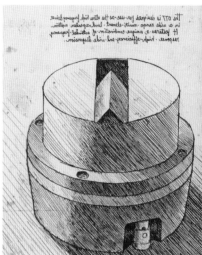

The Horizon 166 made user of a heat-formed plastic mesh grille that resembled a small "egg carton" section. This was also the era of stretch cloth grilles, with wire-form frames as integral parts of the design, as shown in the L65. Designer Arnold Wolf had been among the first to make extensive use of the stretch cloth-plus-wire frame form.

Incidentally, Jubal was a musician mentioned in the Old Testament; the name is obviously a play on the letters "JBL".

L212 Sub-Satellite System

The L212 (1978) was JBL's first venture in the area of subwoofer-satellite systems, a format that eventually hit its stride in the 1990s with the coming of home theater and surround sound. The system consisted of a powered 12-inch subwoofer and 3-way satellites with components in a vertical array. The tight layout of these components, and careful selection of crossover frequencies, resulted in very uniform frequency response and exemplary polar response, as shown in the graph.

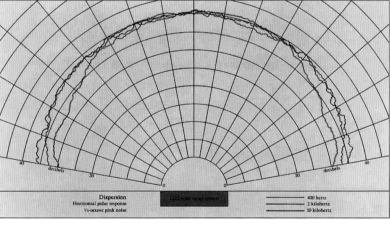

Low Cost Systems from the Late 1970s

JBL introduced the L40 and L50 as lower cost traditional models. The L50, shown at left, was a three-way 10-inch low frequency system with a heat-formed grille with fine felt overlay available in a number of colors. The L40, shown at right, was a two-way ten-inch low frequency system with a simple beveled grille profile.

These systems stressed appearance of the grille rather than baffle componentry, which was soon to become a dominant trend.

Mark Gander was the development engineer for these systems.

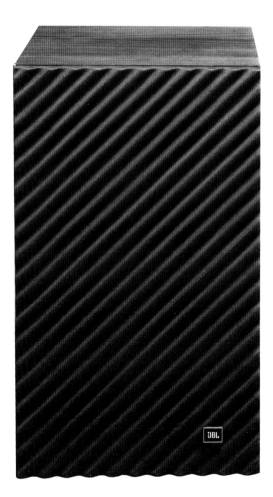

The L220 (1979)

The L220 took a retrospective look back at a time when many new trends were influencing loudspeaker design. The passive radiator (at the bottom of the baffle) harked back to the 1950s; a small folded plate acoustical lens, in the style of the Hartsfield, was placed in front of a cone midrange driver; and a new version of the ring radiator, the model 076, was used for high frequency coverage.

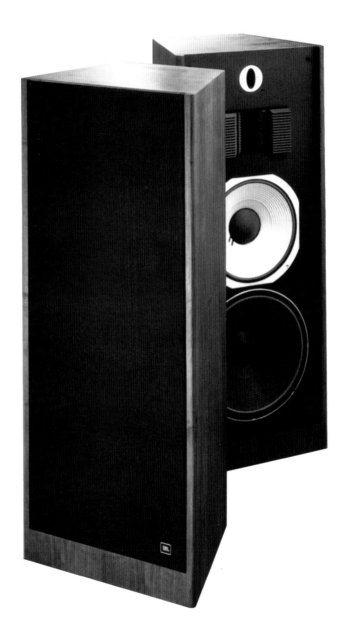

The Ti-Series Products

The development of the titanium dome high frequency driver brought a new level of extended, smooth response to a number of JBL systems. The transducer was fabricated by a proprietary drawing process and incorporated JBL's Diamond Surround. The 250Ti, shown center rear, was a modification of the earlier L250. In one form or another, the L250 remained in the JBL Consumer catalog for nearly two decades.

The JBL XPL-Series

The XPL-Series was introduced in 1989, and with it the 095Ti titanium dome midrange 3-inch driver was first used. The series was especially popular in Europe.

The JBL Lacquer Series (1987)

These striking models are finished in piano quality black polyurethane acrylic enamel in JBL's state of the art enclosure plant. Both industrial design and finish were aimed primarily at the European market.

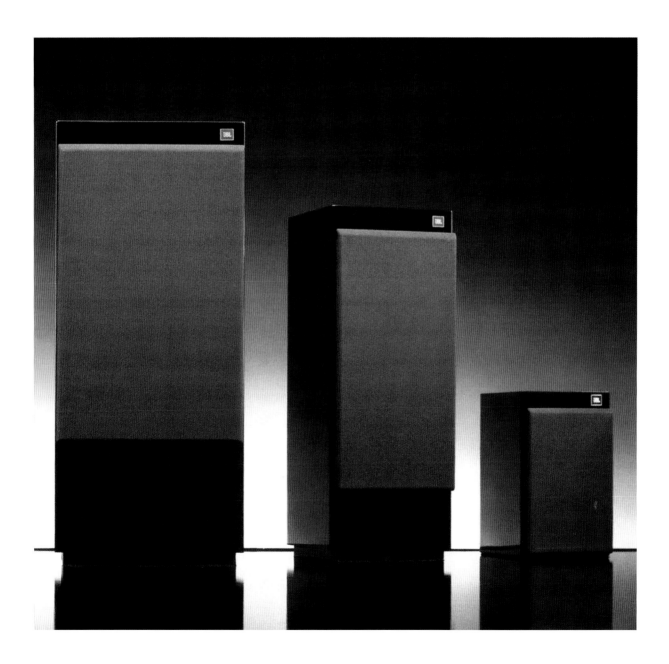

Signature Series, 1988

The Signature Series was JBL's answer to the perennial question of how to furnish the modern home with high quality loudspeaker s that do not take up large amounts of floor space – or otherwise call attention to themselves. The models are S1 through S4, beginning from the left. The S1 is a subwoofer that defies all previous notions of a subwoofer. It is built in a tower configuration and can double as a pedestal. The S2 is a full-range system harking back to the Aquarius 4 of the late 1960s. In a nod to the coming of quality built-in components, S3 and S4 are in-wall units of superior quality.

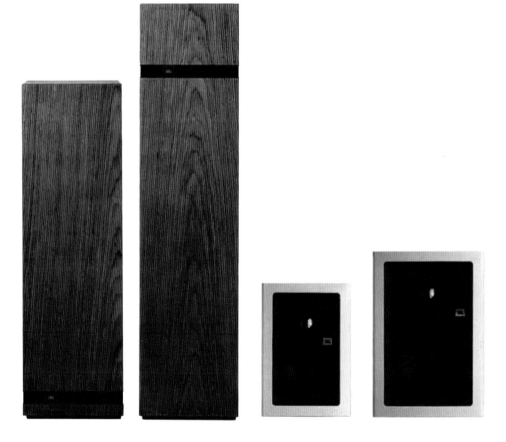

The DD55000 Everest System

As can clearly be seen, the left and right models of the Everest system are mirror images of each other. The asymmetrical mid-frequency horns steer the stereo signals in a cross-firing pattern covering a wide stereo listening area. The "sweet spot" has been eliminated by balancing critical timing cues with compensating amplitude cues.

The Everest was suggested by the late Japanese audio critic Keizo Yamanaka, who first heard the effect of cross-firing the asymmetric horns during a visit to the JBL factory in 1985. Through his efforts and encouragement, the design of the system unfolded, and it was introduced to the Japanese marketplace during the annual Audio Fair. It was the first in a continuing group of flagship products conceived especially for the Japanese high-end consumer market. Dan Ashcraft was the industrial designer of the Everest.

Project K2: Models S9500 and S7500

By 1990 there was need for another flagship product for the Japanese market. Project K2 consisted of a double woofer 2-way system (S9500) and a single woofer 2-way system (S7500). Both models incorporated state of the art transducers, and the overall design execution was truly vintage JBL.

The S9500 is shown in both front and rear views, while a pair of S7500s are shown in another view. Both models rested on a concrete plinth, and the high frequency horn was machined from high density translucent structural plastic. Dan Ashcraft was the industrial designer.

Century Gold, 1996

The Century Gold was a limited edition bookshelf system introduced on the 50th anniversary of JBL in 1996. While JBL's "statement" systems had tended to be large models, the Century Gold harked back to the original Century L100 bookshelf format. It was composed of state of the art components and had uniform frequency and phase response. The enclosure was as rigid as any JBL ever was, and all exposed metal surfaces and finishings were treated with a flash plating of 24-karat gold! It sold out quickly.

TiK Series™, 1999

Breaking out of the rectilinear enclosure design mold has been a difficult thing for the industry to do. The TiK series has done this by using a truncated conical structure with a seam at the back and a flat, sloping baffle at front. A new family of cone low and mid-frequency drivers was developed for these models, and a titanium dome tweeter is used. The larger systems are intended for stereo as well as for left-right use in surround sound systems. The horizontal array is intended as a center channel, and the small 2-way models function very well when stand-mounted for the surround channels.

The Range of Loudspeakers for Home Video

Short of making the move to Synthesis®, which normally requires significant architectural changes, the range of home video is nevertheless quite wide. The upper photo shows the System L. In addition to providing 5.1 surround sound for movies and music on DVD, the two extra channels (not shown in the photo) accommodate the Logic 7 process developed by JBL's sister company, Lexicon. Logic 7 creates an added two channels from information already present in the 5.1 audio stream, creating a truly enveloping sense of space around the listeners. The SCS200.7 system (shown in the inset at the bottom) provides similar response capability on a more modest scale.

Studio L Series Products

The elegant and high-tech Studio L family consists of models intended for both music and home theater. The 4-way designs exhibit both smooth on-axis response and pattern control in both vertical and horizontal planes.

The HT Series™

As indicated by its initials, the HT Series was designed specifically for home theater applications, and the use of a horn high frequency section in a 2-way design is a direct parallel to the screen channel loudspeakers in modern movie theaters. The design followed the THX philosophy for home theater, and matching elements were made for center and surround channel, and subwoofer applications.

Subwoofers, Old and New

The Model B460 (shown at left) was typical of subwoofer designs of the 1990s. It consisted of an 18-inch driver mounted in an 8 cubic foot enclosure ported for a resonance frequency of about 27 Hz. An external amplifier and equalizer were required for its operation. The Model TiK Master Sub (shown at right) is typical of many modern designs. It occupies abut one-third the volume of the B460 and includes integral amplifier/auto-equalization which can be computer controlled. Both systems have roughly the same frequency bandwidth and maximum output capability in the range down to about 30 Hz.

JBL Mid-Level Automotive Products

JBL's mid-level auto products are intended as drop-in replacements for many stock automobile loudspeaker systems as they come off the dealer's lot. These products are sized to fit standard mounting dimensions and come with protective grilles. In most cases the sonic improvements are remarkable.

JBL High-End Automotive Products

JBL addressees high-end automotive needs with a wide variety of transducer components, dividing networks, and power amplifiers. Components of the GTi-Series are shown in this view. For a generation of consumers "on the go," their automotive system may in fact be better than the audio system at home!

Performance Series™ Home Theater Systems

Using newly engineered cone and dome components, the Performance Series offers a set of shallow profile components for wall mounting, tailored for plasma and LCD large-format, high definition home video.

Project Array™ Home Cinema Products

Borrowing from advanced driver technology developed for JBL's flagship products for the high-end Japanese market, the Project Array group uses mid-high and ultra-high frequency horn systems to attain flat response out to 48 kHz. While it is true that nobody can hear these high frequencies as such, there is the technical advantage that in-band signals in the 8 to 16 kHz range will be more accurately reproduced.

Synthesis System® Using Cones and Domes

A Synthesis installation can resemble an actual movie theater. Where flush mounting of loudspeaker components is required, special high-tech Synthesis models specifically designed for the purpose are used. The system shown at left is used for front left and right channels. A similar set of components, arranged horizontally, is used for the center channel and is located above or below the screen. The surround channels use multiples of the model shown above at center. This system permits two modes of surround operation: standard monopole, or THX-recommended dipole use. The system shown at the right is the subwoofer, and may be used in multiples.

Synthesis System Using Cones and Horns

The system shown here is based on the original Synthesis design, which offered the user a horn-type "theater system" for video, along with a more conventional "cone-dome" system for standard stereo listening. These two options can be seen in the mid and high frequency sections of the left-right channels shown at left. These systems also have integral 18-inch subwoofers. The center channel is shown lower right. Surround channels are based on the switchable monopole/dipole arrangement discussed on the previous page.

Synthesis Electronics

A JBL Synthesis installation normally uses JBL electronics which facilitate all aspects of operation, including: program selection, format selection, playback level, and tone control functions. Shown here are two multi-channel amplifiers (middle and lower) and a surround processor/controller (top).

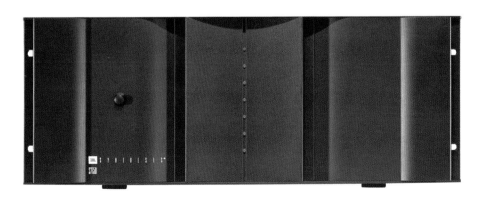

Systems for Computers and Multimedia

These systems are for use on desktops with personal computers. Both have a subwoofer and a left-right pair of satellites. The three systems are powered via amplifiers in the subwoofer module, which normally sits on the floor below the work space. The system shown in the upper panel is whimsically referred to as "Creature®," while the lower one is dubbed "JBL Encounter."

JBL On Stage™ iPod Player

JBL's immensely popular "On Stage" iPod player is designed for docking of the unit when the user is at home. The base is powered by a wall plug-in power supply; the audio output is of high quality and can fill a moderate-size room comfortably.

The trademark On Stage used with permission of OSA international, Inc.

The Control®1 and Control 1X

Since its introduction twenty years ago, the Control 1 has gone through many changes, but remains essentially what it was at the start – a rugged, low-cost, great sounding loudspeaker system with a thousand uses. It has been copied by hundreds of manufacturers, as a casual perusal of your local computer or electronics store will show.

The JBL GTi Automotive Subwoofer

The JBL GTi subwoofer is the only one of its kind. It combines the typical high performance of JBL's pro woofers with the ruggedness and ultra-high output capability demanded for long-term automotive use. The "long-throw" of the cone permits deep bass to be heard in the car's interior, where road noise, with its predominance at low frequencies, can easily mask the program source. Jerry Moro was the transducer design engineer.

K2 S9800 Three-Way System

The K2 S9800 three-way system made use of three new drivers that pushed JBL's already advanced technical envelope even further. Mid-range and ultra-high frequency drivers with beryllium diaphragms were used, and the low frequency driver introduced laminated steel structures in the magnetic circuit to minimize power losses and reduce distortion. The system was introduced to the Japanese high-end market in 2001, followed by introductions in the U. S. and European markets. Greg Timbers was the system design engineer.

Anatomy of a Loudspeaker System: 045Be Ultra High Frequency Driver

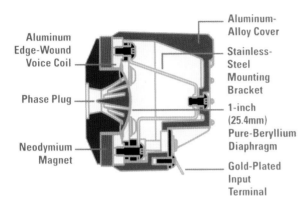

Aluminum Edge-Wound Voice Coil

Phase Plug

Neodymium Magnet

Aluminum-Alloy Cover

Stainless-Steel Mounting Bracket

1-inch (25.4mm) Pure-Beryllium Diaphragm

Gold-Plated Input Terminal

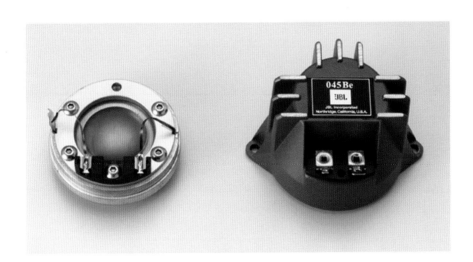

The 045Be driver was designed to enable JBL systems to attain uniform response to 48 kHz, in answer to audiophiles who had acquired SACD and DVD-Audio playback units. A cutaway drawing is shown at upper left. The phase plug, in many ways the heart of the driver, is 1 inch (25 mm) in diameter and is not easily made by modern machining techniques. In this driver, the phase plug is "grown" by a modern process known as stereo lithography – in which all manufactured items are literally clones of the original. The driver mounted on its mating horn is shown at upper right.

The bottom panel shows the rear of the driver with its cover removed. The circular gray element is the beryllium diaphragm, which has a moving mass of a fraction of a gram. The protective rear cover is shown at the right. Tim Prenta was the transducer engineer responsible for the 045Be.

The 045Be is used only in high-end JBL Consumer systems.

Anatomy of a Loudspeaker System: 435Be Midrange Driver and Horn

A section view of the 435Be 3-inch diameter midrange compression driver is shown at upper left, and the driver is shown mounted on its horn at upper right. The bottom panel shows the back cover of the driver (top), and a view of the beryllium diaphragm assembly is shown at lower left. The view at lower right is of the magnetic motor structure, showing the annular slits of the phasing plug and the outer voice coil gap.

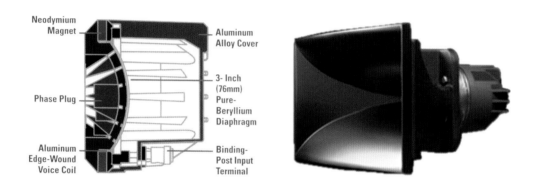

Neodymium Magnet · Aluminum Alloy Cover · Phase Plug · 3-Inch (76mm) Pure-Beryllium Diaphragm · Aluminum Edge-Wound Voice Coil · Binding-Post Input Terminal

Anatomy of a Loudspeaker System: 1500Al Low Frequency Driver

The 1500Al low frequency was designed by Jerry Moro of JBL Consumer's engineering group. Attention was focused on both mechanical and magnetic parameters in an effort to achieve state of the art performance. In the mechanical domain, cone, surround, and inner suspension have all been chosen for the correct combination of mass, stiffness, and internal damping to provide uniform output from the lowest frequencies up to 800 Hz. Magnetic parameters have been adjusted to control gap flux modulation, field uniformity, and eddy-current losses under a wide range of operating conditions.

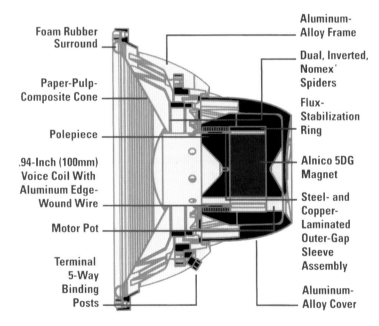

Foam Rubber Surround

Paper-Pulp-Composite Cone

Polepiece

.94-Inch (100mm) Voice Coil With Aluminum Edge-Wound Wire

Motor Pot

Terminal 5-Way Binding Posts

Aluminum-Alloy Frame

Dual, Inverted, Nomex' Spiders

Flux-Stabilization Ring

Alnico 5DG Magnet

Steel- and Copper-Laminated Outer-Gap Sleeve Assembly

Aluminum-Alloy Cover

Anatomy of a Loudspeaker System: Frequency Dividing Network

The dividing network "assigns" input signal frequencies to the appropriate driver. Air core copper coils, along with high quality capacitors and resistors, are used to achieve this, along with adjustment of signal delays in the immediate frequency crossover range to obtain amplitude and phase characteristics that insure uniform response. The net result of this is the response shown in the lower panel.

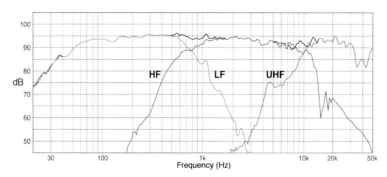

The JBL Everest Model DD66000

The Model 66000 Everest II is the latest entry in the JBL flagship group, and it was introduced in Japan in the Fall of 2006. The stunning industrial design is the work of Dan Ashcraft, who has played a commanding role in JBL Consumer product design for more than twenty years.

Greg Timbers was the system design engineer, and Jerry Moro was responsible for both the low frequency driver and the new 476Be 4-inch beryllium diaphragm midrange compression driver. Tim Prenta's 1-inch ultra-high frequency unit is also an essential element in this system.

Chapter 5: Monitors for Recording and Broadcast

Lansing's first monitor loudspeaker was the Iconic, a product from the 1930s that set the basic direction that all big monitors have taken: a direct radiator low frequency section and a horn-loaded high frequency section. When JBL was formed in 1946, it took almost two decades for the company to reintroduce a dedicated monitor into the line. Combining an LE-Series low frequency section with a slant plate acoustical lens, engineer Bart Locanthi produced a special model for Capitol Records in 1963. This landmark system was subsequently relabeled 4320, and it spawned the renowned 4300-Series products that were popular throughout the 1970s.

During the early 1980s, taking advantage of the recently minted flat power response concept, the 4400-Series models were introduced, once again introducing the notion the 2-way monitor approach at JBL.

As we approached the 1990s, digital recording was firmly in place, and digital audio work stations were finding their way into home studio environments. Large monitor sales were flagging as many smaller monitors came on the market. JBL's recent efforts here have met with great success. The LSR (Linear Spatial Reference) concept describes products that have not only flat on-axis response, but also controlled off-axis response. More recent models have integral equalization for room matching, and the most recent small monitors, the LSR4300-Series, carry out the equalization function automatically.

The Lansing "Iconic" System
The First Studio Monitor

In 1938, Jim Lansing introduced the Iconic 2-way loudspeaker system as a monitor to be used in screening and review rooms for the motion picture industry. It consisted of a moderate efficiency low frequency driver with a small multicellular horn/driver combination operating from about 800 Hz upward. In those days before high-energy magnets, a dc power supply was necessary to establish a sufficiently high magnetic flux field to achieve the desired response.

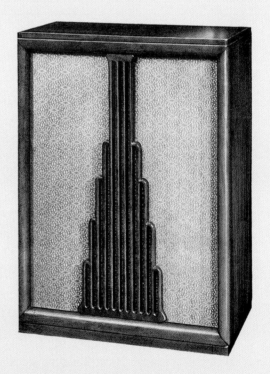

How little things have changed in 70 years. Today's low frequency drivers are still used in ported enclosures, while the multicellular horn was replaced, first with acoustic lenses and later, with high frequency horns designed as waveguides. Biamplification has become a standard practice, and high energy magnets have become commonplace.

The utility system shown at the left was the standard for early studios. The version shown at the right, with its Art Deco motifs, was intended for home use as well as in the executive suite.

An Offer from JBL
(circa 1959)

Even though JBL had never manufactured the Iconic, its components were similar enough in size and performance to enable a functional retrofit. The gesture of an unlimited warranty was one basically of good will on the part of William Thomas in memory of the accomplishments of Jim Lansing during the 1930s.

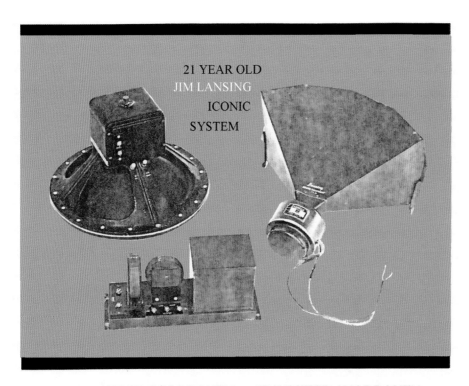

21 YEAR OLD
JIM LANSING
ICONIC
SYSTEM

STILL UNDER WARRANTY... UNLIMITED WARRANTY

It is – and always has been – JBL's policy to repair or replace *without charge*, at any time during the life of the product, any unit whose performance is impaired by a cause or causes beyond the control of the owner. The only limitation is the availability of parts. Frequently, as in the Iconic system shown above, it is possible to use today's parts in discontinued models. For a generation this fine Jim Lansing system provided listening pleasure of a very high order to its owner. Then it became apparent that all was not well. Having obtained permission, the owner packed the system off to the factory for repairs.

Replacement parts, re-assembly, and testing were provided *without charge*. The system now sounds better than it did when new. This is another reason why the astute music lover invests in the finest loudspeakers he can find. Like any fine musical instrument, they don't wear out, are almost always worth restoring to top-notch playing condition. Read the JBL warranty lately? There are three provisos especially interesting to the Audio Specialist.

1. The warranty is effective only if the speaker was purchased from a Franchised JBL Dealer. **2.** Before any equipment is returned to the factory, the owner must notify the dealer who sold it to him. **3.** No equipment will be received at the factory unless prior written authorization has been issued by the factory. Show the warranty card to your customers. It makes a very strong selling point.

*JBL precision transducers are manufactured by **JAMES B. LANSING SOUND, INC.**, and are marketed by **JBL INTERNATIONAL**, Los Angeles 39, California*

The JBL 4320 Studio Monitor

Originally designed for Capitol Records in Hollywood, the 4320 was first designated as the C50SMS7 system. It was introduced in 1963, and it soon became a standard monitor within the EMI Recording corporate structure worldwide. Subsequent 3-way versions were produced. The familiar cream grey spackle finish of the enclosure supported a light mesh grille, later to be replaced by the black stretch fabric version shown here. The wide side relief features of the grille were necessary to accommodate the ±80-degree radiation characteristics of the horn/lens combination.

Acoustically, the combination of a woofer with smooth response up to about 800 Hz and a horn/lens combination extending the response uniformly beyond 15 kHz was almost ideal. Each exhibited flat on-axis response over its bandwidth, and the dividing network was virtually "from the textbook" in its simplicity.

Much of the success of the 4320 lay in the simple fact that it was an integral system which included a dedicated enclosure that was optimum in both volume and tuning. At the time it was making its ascendancy in the industry, both the Altec 604 and the Tannoy Gold, the other two major contenders for first place, were sold as individual drivers. As such, they were mounted in a wide variety of enclosures with various volumes and tunings, and with little regard for optimum system low frequency alignment.

The First JBL Bookshelf Monitors: 4310 and 4311

At the request of Robert Fine, noted New York recording engineer, JBL developed the 3-way bookshelf monitor that eventually became the 4310. The year was 1967, and Fine had just outfitted his famous studio in the Great Northern Hotel with 8-track recording capability. He needed 8 small but robust monitors to fit over the control room window. The "half-moon" baffle standoff in the 4310 was intended to minimize boundary irregularities when the grille was in place. Subsequent measurements showed that this was not necessary and the 4311 model dispensed with that detail. The 4311 also rearranged the drivers into a tighter cluster. The 4311 and its consumer cousin, the Century L100, became bestsellers for JBL during the early to mid-1970s.

JBL 4300-Series Monitors
Decade of the 1970s

The decade of the 1970s saw a proliferation of JBL monitors, most of them making use of the small slant-plate acoustic lens and slot-type high frequency ring radiator. Clockwise from upper left: 4313B 3-way; 4333B 3-way; 4331B 2-way; and 4343B 4-way. The 4350 4-way is shown in the bottom photo.

The monitor market surge of the 1970s was driven by two factors: all JBL monitors had a dedicated enclosure, with its carefully adjusted volume and tuning alignment for optimum performance. The second factor was the unexpected popularity of these systems in the Japanese and Southeast Asian high fidelity markets. As an example, the dual-woofer 4350 was introduced at a time when the recording industry was looking for increased broadband output capability at a time when neither Altec nor Tannoy had tackled the enclosure problem.

Bi-Radial® Studio Monitors

The JBL Bi-Radial monitors provided uniform horizontal and vertical coverage over the frequency range from 800 to 12 kHz, creating a reflected sound field in the control room that was both uniform and neutral. These 2-way systems were essentially aligned in their time domain response, and they brought the concept of uniform power response into the studio for the first time. The single 15-inch 4430 is shown at bottom left, while the dual 15-inch 4435 is at bottom right. The smaller 12-inch 4425 is at the upper right.

These systems are shown here in their floor-standing orientations, and as such they exhibit a 10-degrees upward launch angle at the crossover frequency of 1 kHz. When these models are soffit-mounted, maintaining the same orientation, the high frequency section is normally "flipped" so the effective launch angle is then minus 10 degrees in the vertical plane.

LSR (Linear Spatial Reference) Modern Mid-Field Monitor Systems

The original LSR-Series monitors are shown in the upper panel. The term LSR describes the uniformity of both on-axis and overall power response of these systems. The LSR32P (upper left) was a heavy duty passive system capable of substantial output. The LSR28P (center) was a self-powered biamplified system, and the LSR12SP (upper right) was a powered subwoofer.

The lower panel shows the three models in the reduced-size category LSR4300-Series: the LSR4326P (left), the LSR4328P (center), and the LSR4312SP (right). These models are digitally integrated to achieve remote control of level, room and boundary equalization, program source selection, as well as format selection – all visible on a computer screen. This series is aimed primarily at modern audio work stations in a variety of smaller environments.

JBL LSR28P Monitors in Near-Field Application at Sound Chamber Recorders North Hollywood, CA

LSR28P monitors are shown in a left, center, right configuration on the console meter bridge in the control room at Sound Chamber Recorders. The studio is seen through the window. What we call nearfield monitoring has changed over the years. At one time the term referred to a small pair of limited bandwidth loudspeakers so that the engineer and producer could make an early judgment of what the recorded product might sound like in an automobile, or via a small home system. There have been enough improvements in both home and automotive systems to force a paradigm change, and today we routinely see full-bandwidth systems on the meter bridge.

Cherokee Studios
Hollywood, CA

Cherokee Studios has long been a mainstay of recording in Los Angeles and is a long-time user of JBL monitors. The custom soffit-mounted design by George Augspurger is shown in the center channel position above the control room window. On the meter bridge of the console is the JBL LSR6328P system.

The National Academy of Recording Arts and Sciences
Santa Monica, CA

The Recording Academy has an extensive JBL playback system in its board of Directors meeting room. In this photo, left, center, and right channels of a multichannel systems are shown. The left and right main loudspeakers are JBL LSR6332 systems, each with a pair of LSR6312SP powered subwoofers, over and under the full-range systems. The center channel is a custom design mounted over the rear projection screen. Four surround loudspeakers are flush mounted into columns, two on each side of the room, and can be used either in a conventional 5.1 channel playback mode or a 7.1 expanded mode. Normally, the front channels are covered by black stretch cloth grilles, which have been removed here to show details of the installation. Photograph by Peter Chaikin.

Filipetti and Ramone remixing "Graceland"

The multichannel tracks for Paul Simon's celebrated "Graceland" album are in the process of being remixed to 5.1 surround sound. Award winning engineer Frank Filipetti (left) and producer Phil Ramone (right) are shown here, clearly enjoying what they are doing.

Frank Filipetti began his career as a musician, eventually making his way into production and engineering. He is a leading engineer in the area of high-end audio remixing of recent, as well as legacy, program material for surround sound release.

Phil Ramone rose to prominence in the 1960s as one of the principals of A and R Recording in New York. He has made a very successful transition from engineer to producer and has been busy in album production ever since.

JBL LSR6328P loudspeakers are shown in front, center, and right positions; rear channel loudspeakers and subwoofers are out of view.

Mi Casa Studios, Hollywood, CA

Mi Casa is a much in demand remix facility in Hollywood specializing in 5.1 mixdowns for both film and music clients. Mi Casa was there when surround sound was introduced, and they are responsible for many of the remixes of legacy multichannel product originally released only in stereo. In recent years they have broadened their work to include surround up-mixes for the motion picture industry. JBL LSR28P systems are shown here in front, center, and right positions. The rear channels are out of the picture, as are the subwoofers.

LSR Systems at Image Resources Post Production, Encino, CA

Image Resources is typical of many Los Angeles audio and video post-production operations that have moved into a suburban setting, where things are quieter and the parking easier. The photograph shows one of their larger video rooms, with the perforated screen at the right and a pair of surrounds (LSR6328P) mounted on the left side wall. Three LSR6332Ps and a single 4645C 18-inch subwoofer are located behind the screen. Additional pairs of LSR6328Ps are positioned on the back and right side walls. Mark Noad and Dave Moorman are the principals of the company.

Acoustics and design were carried out by Carl Yancher of Studio Design, Foothill Ranch, CA, and construction was carried out by DP Builders, Los Angeles. Photograph by Evan McKenzie.

Chapter 6: Systems for Motion Pictures

When JBL made its return to the motion picture market in the early 1980s, we were in a sense reclaiming old territory. After all, it was the Shearer-Lansing theater system of the 1930s that put Jim Lansing in the Professional loudspeaker business in the first place. The improvements in response uniformity that characterized the new JBL systems were broadly accepted by both the exhibition industry and the Hollywood creative community, and you will find JBL theater products in showcase exhibition houses as well as professional installations around the world. For some years, JBL has been the number one supplier of loudspeakers for the movie industry worldwide.

Jim Lansing's work with MGM and Douglas Shearer has been well documented elsewhere in this book, and it is an important piece of cinema history. What is not generally known is the work that JBL did in the early 1950s, at the onset of motion picture stereo, for such companies as Ampex and Westrex. The development of large format acoustic lenses, JBL's early series of radial horns, and the 375 large format compression driver were central to these enterprises. These products also served to put JBL on the map, so to speak, as a major player not only in cinema but in commercial and professional sound in general.

We begin this section with an early JBL advertisement from the 1950s, moving on to a survey of earlier JBL systems designed for motion picture use. We conclude with a brief survey of modern showcase installations.

JBL's First Theater System

The system shown in this advertisement is basically the same as that which John Frayne of Westrex and Bart Locanthi of JBL designed for Westrex, the export division of Western Electric. JBL had retained the rights to the design, and when the Westrex effort was discontinued JBL reintroduced the system domestically.

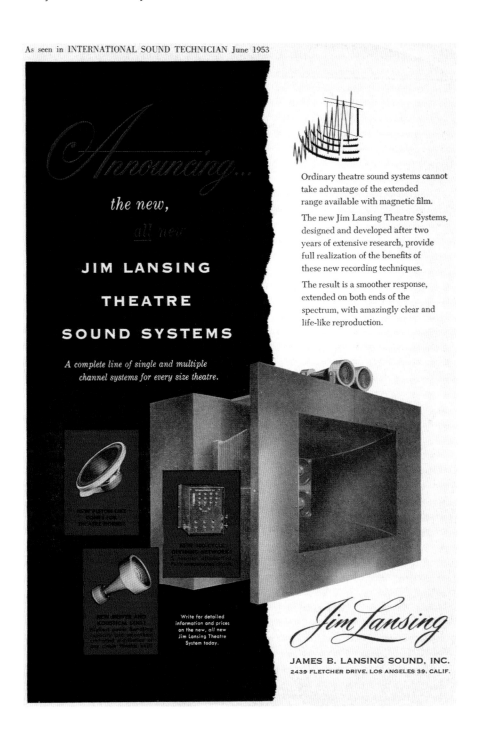

JBL Earlier-Style Theater Systems, 1979–1982

Before the introduction of the flat power concept in motion picture loudspeaker design, JBL's theater models were fairly typical of the earlier Altec Lansing era. These systems made use basically of low frequency ported horn sections topped off by a radial horn. At this time JBL was a minor player in the film exhibition market.

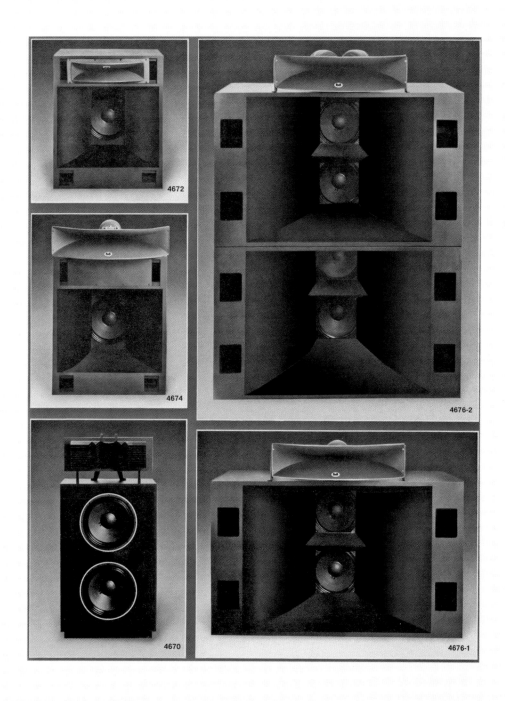

The First Cinema System with Flat Power Response

946 mm
(37.25")

1453 mm
(57.19")

2215 mm
(87.19")

451 mm
(17.75")

Details of the JBL 4675 cinema system loudspeaker are shown here. The 2360 Bi-Radial horn provides a uniform 90°-by-40° coverage pattern from 500 Hz to about 12 kHz. At the 500-Hz crossover point, the dual 15-inch direct radiator low frequency section has a pattern which matches that of the high frequency within a directivity index of ±1.5 dB. The low frequency pattern control extends downward to about 125 Hz, providing an overall two-decade-wide frequency range over which it is possible to achieve both uniform axial response and total radiated power response. More details on the flat power response concept are given in Chapter 2.

The 5000-Series Three-Way Theater Systems

Developed in cooperation with the Motion Picture Academy's Theater Standards Committee in the late 1990s, the 5000-Series products introduced the first three-way design intended for cinema application since the early 1930s. The primary driving force was the introduction of digital sound tracks with their very low levels of distortion. Dividing the normal system bandwidth into 3 ranges, instead of the traditional 2, was the only way to minimize distortion during the playback process. A new high frequency compression driver was developed for this application, as well as a large-format specialized driver for the midrange, and triamplification was used with the screen channels. System variants are available with one, two, and four 15-inch woofers, the latter in a "diamond Quad" arrangement.

ScreenArray® Theater Loudspeakers

The ScreenArray loudspeakers were developed to address a number of modern theater design considerations that dictated a need for a new standard in cinema loudspeaker performance. Depth behind the screen is increasingly more limited, and the new ScreenArray design traded the large mid-frequency horns for a line array of horn-loaded midrange drivers that can deliver more output with lower distortion. Stadium seating required special attention to audience coverage, and patented Focused Coverage Technology, via the frequency dividing network, gives these arrays more uniform vertical pattern control. Additionally, the slight vertical asymmetry of the high frequency horn tilts the radiation pattern downward by about 10 degrees to match that of the midrange section, providing optimum coverage. The high frequency horn also compensates for frequency dispersive spreading caused by the perforated screen.

ScreenArray systems are available for biamplified operation. Triamplified is optional for THX certification and for highest performance. In March 2002, the Academy of Motion Picture Arts and Sciences presented JBL engineers with a Technical Achievement Award "for the engineering and design of filtered line arrays and screen spreading compensation as applied to motion picture loudspeaker systems," as employed in these ScreenArray systems.

Grauman's Chinese Theater
Hollywood, CA

Sid Grauman's Chinese Theater was built in 1927 and is one of Hollywood's acknowledged icons. The Chinese is now owned by Mann Theatres. During the 1930s it was equipped with an original Shearer-Lansing system, but today it has five JBL custom ScreenArray systems behind the screen, 12 JBL subwoofers, and a large complement of 42 surround loudspeakers. Once-troublesome acoustics have in recent years been modified, and today the Chinese is much in demand for film premiers. The associated multiplex installations are also outfitted with JBL ScreenArray systems.

Samuel Goldwyn Theater at the Academy of Motion Picture Arts and Sciences Beverly Hills, CA

Since 1984 there has been a JBL system in the prestigious Goldwyn Theater of the Motion Picture Academy. The present system, shown in the upper photo, consists of five 5674 three-way systems positioned in a solid baffle wall. The lower photo shows the first 1984 installation, consisting of 4675 2-way models.

The present Academy systems also contains a surround array of 24 custom loudspeakers flushed into the side and rear walls behind scrim. Earlier in 2006, an all-new array of sixteen 18-inch subwoofers was installed below the screen channels at floor level.

"Academy Award" and "Oscar" image ©AMPAS®

Marounuchi Plaza, Tokyo

Marounuchi Plaza is typical of new cinema design in Japan. The theater seats about 1000 patrons and has model 5674 3-way screen systems. You will note that the surround loudspeakers are doubled, one over the other, making a total of 36 surrounds. This theater typifies the current state of new cinema design in Japan.

The Goldenson Theater, Academy of Television Arts and Sciences North Hollywood, CA

The Goldenson Theater of the Academy of Television Arts and Sciences in North Hollywood, CA, has an installation consisting of 5 JBL custom Screen-Array systems, an ensemble of twelve 18-inch subwoofers, and 12 custom surround systems. The impressive photo shown here is of all 5 screen channels, along with a view of one of the "Emmy" statues, the emblem of the Academy. The photo was taken just prior to installing the screen and shows in detail the scope of the loudspeaker wall and its acoustical treatment. The Goldenson is one of the major professional film/TV exhibit houses in the greater Los Angeles Area. Architectural and acoustical design were carried out by Jeff Cooper Architects, AIA, Los Angeles, CA.

Directors Guild of America Hollywood, CA

Along with the Motion Picture and Television Academies, the Directors Guild is one of the "big three" professional motion picture theaters in the greater Los Angeles area. There are three theaters at the Directors Guild, all of them outfitted with JBL loudspeakers. In Theater 1, shown here, 5 screen channels of three-way systems are complemented with 8 subwoofers and 24 surround loudspeakers. The photograph shows the system just prior to the installation of the screen. Architectural and acoustical design were carried out by Jeff Cooper Architects, AIA, Los Angeles, CA.

Marcus Fox Ultrascreen Theatre
Elgin, IL

This cinema installation features Digital B-Chain, a signal-routing protocol developed by JBL Professional and its sister company Crown International. It represents a major step forward in the art and science of digital sound in the motion picture theater. With DBC, all audio and control signals remain in the digital domain, requiring only a single ethernet connection.

Audio and Video Monitoring with Theater Components

Reaching for the very best, the television broadcasting center shown here chose to monitor its programs via high-end JBL screen channel components. This German production center uses a perforated screen, along with three ScreenArray 3632 models and 8340A surrounds. In the lower photo, backlighting makes the loudspeakers visible through the perforated screen.

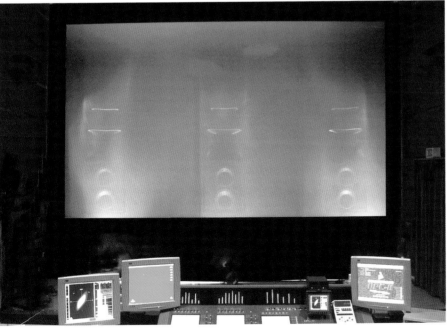

The Bridge Cinema De Lux
West Los Angeles

The Bridge is a sumptuous new 17 screen National Amusements Theatre on the West Side with JBL components throughout. The Director's Hall is a special venue featuring extra wide seats and reserved seating. In a review of L. A. theaters, the Los Angeles Times reported that the Bridge is one of the top three "best sounding movie theaters in Los Angeles." The other two were the Pacific Cinerama Dome and Arclight Theatres, also JBL installations.

The Mann Theaters in Westwood Village Los Angeles

Mann's Westwood and Bruin Theaters on the West Side of Los Angeles are two of the city's favorites. The Bruin, named after the nearby UCLA football team, is relatively recent, but the Westwood dates back to the glory days when studios built and owned their own theaters. Both houses have JBL 4675 systems, plus subwoofers and large surround arrays.

The Cinerama Dome, Pacific Theatre's Arclight Hollywood, CA

The Cinerama Dome was built in the 1960s as a premier showcase theater for Cinerama exhibition. While Cinerama did not last, the "Dome" remains a Hollywood showcase venue and continues as the site of many premiers. Recent acoustical treatment has solved the problems inherent in domed spaces, and with the installation of JBL custom ScreenArray screen channel systems, complete with an array of 48 surrounds, this venue is now considered one of the finest in town. Almost as an afterthought, the Dome was outfitted earlier in this decade with complete Cinerama projection and sound equipment, and original Cinerama prints are shown at regular intervals. The surrounding multiplex cinema installations are also JBL equipped. Photos courtesy Pacific Theatres.

JBL at the Alfred Hitchcock Theatre
Universal Studios, Universal City, CA

For nearly two decades, Universal's showcase Alfred Hitchcock Theatre has had JBL loudspeakers, and the tradition continues with the current 5000 Series installation. The facility is used as a mixing studio as well as a screening theatre. Architectural and acoustical design were carried out by Jeff Cooper Architects, AIA, Los Angeles. Photo courtesy Universal Studios.

Chapter 7: Portable Systems for Music and Speech

A large segment of the music profession relies on portable systems for all kinds of reinforcement work, ranging from a single vocal or instrumental application to the requirements for a group of players.

It was Leo Fender who, in the 1950s, virtually invented the electric guitar. His search for better loudspeakers brought him to JBL, and we have been makers of speakers for musicians ever since. What guitar player hasn't coveted a JBL speaker?

Over the years, many of Jim Lansing's early transducer models, such as the D130 and D131, have lived on in the JBL Professional line through subsequent F, K, and E Series models. Other specific models have been developed for the musician as well, and we will include them under the major heading of portable products.

In the mid-1970s JBL introduced the Cabaret Series, our first family of products for this purpose. Since that time, the MI (Musical Instrument) area has burgeoned, and there have been many improvements in performance. Today's VRX Series products have brought the performance attributes of line arrays to this area as well.

We will discuss a number of model groups in detail, including the ground-breaking EON family, and we will again give our respects to JBL's long-time friend Les Paul, whose association with our products goes all the way back to Jim Lansing in the early 1940s.

Les Paul Remembers...

The renowned Les Paul first met Jim Lansing in the early 1940s and had this to say about him, "There were three or four people in the loudspeaker business that I'd rub elbows with and none of them – none of them – even approached what I was looking for until I got with Jim Lansing . . . Every kid in a rock band today has to thank Jim Lansing. What he did absolutely made it possible for the musician to get very close reproduction of what he wished to hear."

MUSICAL INSTRUMENT
LOUDSPEAKERS FROM JBL

PUBLICATION GC65

JBL D110F

JBL D120F

JBL D130F

JBL D140F

F-SERIES

Professional musicians are always searching for ways to improve their instruments. And the top artists throughout the world have discovered that JBL loudspeakers provide a brilliance of tone, dynamic range and reliability which is not available with any other speaker, regardless of price or size. And no wonder . . . these are the first professional-quality speakers designed for use with electric musical instruments!

Their unique engineering features and careful craftsmanship provide the amazing "JBL sound": honest bass, sharp mid-range, bright smooth treble, instantaneous response, and effortless total sound. "Look for the F!" The F at the end of the model number tells you that the loudspeaker is expressly designed for use with electrical musical instruments.

The "F" in this early-1960s advertisement originally stood for Fender, the first company for which JBL made special loudspeakers for musical instrument (MI) applications. In time, JBL offered these products to the MI market at large, and the "F" designation was retained. The descendents of these models were known as the K Series, and then as the E series.

The JBL 4882 "Strong Box" Line Array

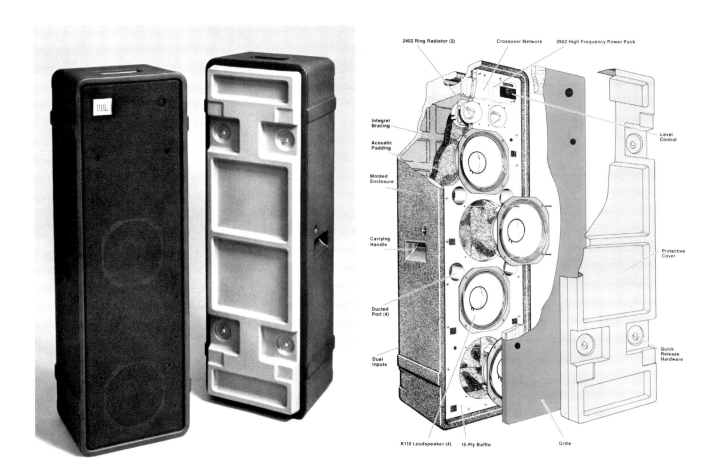

During the mid-1970s JBL developed the 4682 line array for heavy duty performance in portable music applications. In order to hold up under all kinds of potential abuse on the road, the enclosure was made of structural urethane foam. The material was both lighter and stronger than plywood, and the enclosure was also provided with a protective mating front cover.

The componentry consisted of four equally spaced K110 10-inch drivers, topped off at the highest frequencies by a pair of 2402 UHF drivers, to produce sound reinforcement capable of cutting through high ambient noise levels often found in clubs and cabarets.

When used in its normal vertical position, the system had a wide horizontal radiation pattern and a narrow vertical pattern to match the basic requirements of the traditional environments it was used in.

The JBL 4662 and 4663 Systems

During the 1970s it was customary for many users to assemble their own systems for a variety of music and speech reinforcement applications. By making a slight change in the structure of the 4560 horn loaded 15-inch woofer enclosure, JBL made it possible to front-mount the 2345 radial horn in the upper part of the enclosure. A K130 was used as the woofer for maximum output. This system was offered by JBL in both a 2-way configuration (4662) and in a 3-way configuration (4663) that included a 2405 UHF transducer for extended high-end output. It provided an early attempt at a packaged, portable PA system. The later "A" versions upgraded to a 2370 Flat-Front Bi-Radial horn and substituted an E140 woofer for greater power handling and ruggedness.

The JBL Cabaret Series

Introduced in 1979, the Cabaret Series was the first line of packaged JBL systems to provide high performance and portability. It gave the performing musician the features of handles, industrial grade finish, protective baffle covers, and corner protectors. The corner protectors also provided an interlocking feature that allowed multiple enclosures to be stacked one atop the other. The use of multi-layer cross-grain plywood ensured the ruggedness and longevity of these systems.

In addition to these features, the specific models in the series had been defined in terms of the minimum number of products that would accommodate the major needs of a typical modern performing group. First introduced with K-Series Musical Instrument loudspeakers, and soon upgraded to the new SFG E-Series, the line included two lead guitar models, a single model for acoustic guitar or vocal, bass guitar, keyboard, a line array for reinforcement, and finally a stage monitor.

It was in fact the company's first venture in a direction that has become a standard in JBL's product development and in the industry at large. Later additions to the line would take advantage of Bi-Radial horns and tweeters, and focus on sound reinforcement in all shapes and sizes of enclosures and system configurations. Mark Gander was the development engineer for these systems.

Cabaret Series

Some people think our Cabaret Series is too expensive.

In 1959, some people thought this guitar was too.

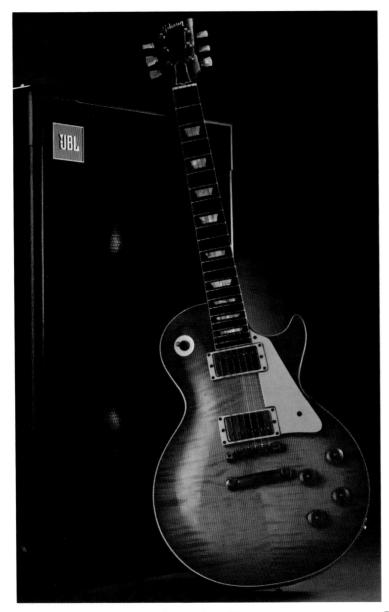

In 1959, this Gibson Les Paul Standard carried a suggested list price of $283. An amount that many considered outrageous for an electric guitar. Yet for those who could appreciate the value in the guitar's craftsmanship, tone, and playability, the price was more than justified.

Today, the JBL Cabaret Series could be considered too expensive. But like the classic Les Paul, Cabaret products are designed to deliver unsurpassed performance. Performance ensured by premium E Series musical instrument loudspeakers, rugged, optimally tuned enclosures, and painstaking attention to detail. All of which help the Cabaret Series offer an additional feature that you might not have thought about—one of the highest resale values in the industry.

So before you buy a new sound system, ask your JBL dealer for a demonstration of the Cabaret Series. It may cost a little more, but the best investments usually do.

James B. Lansing Sound, Inc.,
8500 Balboa Boulevard,
P.O. Box 2200,
Northridge, California 91329 U.S.A.

1959 Gibson Les Paul Standard "Sunburst" serial number 9 0823 courtesy of Norman's Rare Guitars, Reseda, California.

See the complete line of Cabaret Series guitar, bass, keyboard, and vocal reinforcement systems at your JBL dealer.

 **Professional Products Division**

Available in Canada through Gould Marketing. Montréal. Québec.   JBL / harman international

Sound Power Series

In the late 1980s, JBL created a product line for the European market which combined the success of the Cabaret Series with the newer componentry and some of the system configurations of the tour sound Concert Series. The Sound Power Series was a success with performers in clubs and auditoriums, as well as in portable traveling use. Subsequent versions included separate variations for Tour, Install, and Portable applications with different combinations of handles, suspension fixtures and other features.

The JBL MR Series

The MR Series was introduced in the 1990s and was targeted at traveling musicians and disc jockeys. The models were designed to match the characteristics of various instruments and instrumental groups in terms of frequency response and output requirements. Two models of stage monitors were provided. A new line of 3-inch voice coil cone transducers was developed for this series, as well as a smaller Flat-Front Bi-Radial horn and cost-effective compression driver. The success of the price and performance of the product line led to the succession of MR800 through MR900 to the MPro Series.

President Bill Clinton at JBL, 1996

As the guest of Chairman Sidney Harman and JBL, President Clinton gave a talk to the combined workforce of JBL and Harman plants in Northridge – a day of honor and opportunity for our employees to meet with and ask questions of the country's Chief Executive.

Two built-in amplifiers—one for the woofer and one for the tweeter. The result—while the bass is pounding, the high frequencies and vocals are crisp and clear.

Passive crossovers waste as much as half of the amplifier power by generating heat. EON Powered Speakers have built-in active crossovers that use the amplifier power to produce more of what you want—SOUND.

Heat is the #1 enemy of loudspeakers. EON has a die-cast aluminum baffle that absorbs heat away from the woofer and amps and quickly dissipates it to keep them running cool. The more you crank it, the better the system works.

The highly durable and versatile EON polypropylene enclosure allows the speaker to stand upright, tilt back for stage monitor use, hang on a wall or mount on a tripod speaker stand.

EON's flattened voice coil wire allows for 22% more wire in the magnetic gap than most speakers using round wire. More wire = higher efficiency = plays louder.

Patented Differential Drive™ results in a woofer that weighs less than 3 lbs, yet plays louder than similar woofers weighing in at more than 16 lbs! More power, more punch... less weight.

JBL Professional's low mass titanium diaphragm provides extended high frequency for sharper transients. Lighter mass = higher efficiency = You can play louder.

New, low-distortion Bi-Radial® horn provides smooth high frequency coverage so you'll sound as good in the cheap seats as you do up front.

Built-in thermal protection. If the amplifiers overheat, they shut themselves off before any damage can be done—and we guarantee it!

Aluminum fins cast into the ports provide active cooling to the whole system. The louder you play, the more it cools!!

EON woofer cones are computer-designed using Finite Element Analysis techniques to develop a lightweight cone without sacrificing strength.

Neodymium magnets are ten times lighter yet yield the same strength as the conventional ferrite magnets used by our competitors.

Torroidal transformer powers the amplifiers without adding excessive weight. EON Powered Speakers —the lightest in their class.

THE MOST IMPORTANT THING TO LOOK FOR

Need more? Every EON Powered Speaker has features such as an XLR input for easy connection...a peak indicator that alerts the operator before a problem starts...a button that gives you instant PA when you plug in your microphone...a daisy chain output jack that gives your sound system room to grow...and an ergonomic carrying handle mounted at the center of gravity.

EON® JBL

EVEN AN EON POWERED SPEAKER CAN'T GET BY ON GOOD LOOKS ALONE.

SOUND THAT CARRIES

H A Harman International Company

©1996 JBL Professional

The JBL SRX700 Series

Along more modern lines, the JBL SRX700 Series products include the many improvements JBL has made for the traveling musician: Duraflex™ coated enclosures with high quality birch construction, Differential Drive® woofers and neodymium magnets for high output with low weight, and scuff-resistant 16-gauge grilles.

The JBL VRX900 Series

The VRX900 products incorporate the advantages of VerTec in a smaller size suitable for portable use. The basic unit can be arrayed in arc form as shown, and for most portable applications no more than two or three units may be required. A subwoofer is optional, and, as shown, a dual element array can be suspended on a pole over the subwoofer. These models are often used in permanent installations in moderate-size rooms.

Chapter 8: Tour Sound and Special Events

JBL has been a major player in the tour sound market since its inception at the birth of rock and roll. By the 1960s, major tour sound rental companies were coming onto the scene and assumed responsibility for sound, lighting, and other aspects of stagecraft for artists on tour. For the most part these companies assembled their own proprietary systems, usually from JBL components, and developed the necessary custom electronics, travel cases and rigging and suspension hardware to enable a show to be readily transported and quickly go together at a show or festival site in a matter of hours. Environmental conditions, rapidly-changing schedule and logistical conditions and large audiences have given rise to special tools and techniques in order for traveling crews of technicians to meet the high quality expectations of demanding performers.

As new developments in high-performance component transducer and loudspeaker array technology have emerged, so has tour sound technology evolved. Dedicated stage monitoring systems for performing artists, multi-pair signal cabling ('snakes') with quick connect-disconnect facilities, and loudspeaker products with integrated suspension hardware fittings have all been developed first for use in the fast-paced world of tour sound. Developments in the field of tour sound have subsequently influenced system design trends in the larger and somewhat more conservative market for installed venue systems.

There has long been engineering-oriented communication between JBL and the major tour companies, enabling JBL to design and build systems that are specific for the tasks at hand. The early component-assembled systems, through Concert Series, HLA (Horn Loaded Array), and, most recently, VerTec line arrays, were all engineered with specific input from our major users.

In this chapter we will review some of the product groups that have been used in tour sound activities. These will be followed by the earliest examples of concert sound reinforcement, then move on to modern examples of the craft.

Radial Horns and Bass Bins

In the late 1960s and early 1970s, JBL's high efficiency hardware consisted primarily of radial horns and front-loaded, ported bass horns, commonly referred to as bass bins. The single 15-inch model 4560 and dual 15-inch model 4550 were designed to maximize output from the cone transducer as well as fit through doorways — and be able to be efficiently produced from a sheet of plywood. The radials were based around the 2350 90° model using either the 2440 4-inch aluminum diaphragm compression driver or the 2482 driver with a more rugged phenolic resin-impregnated linen diaphragm. These building blocks were often used in large numbers in order to reach the desired sound pressure levels. At the time there was no such thing as "arrayability," and assembling the system was essentially little more than stacking one element on top of another. Still, the audiences came and asked for more.

This photo is of the "Alabama State Troopers" tour, with the componentry developed and field tested with Swanson Sound of Oakland, CA.

The Concert Series

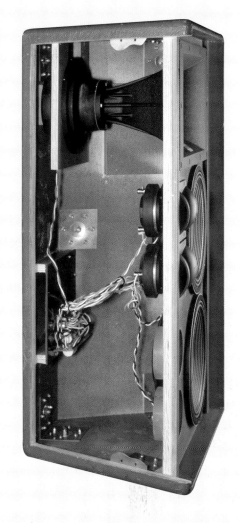

In the mid 1980s JBL developed the Concert Series, which consisted of full-range systems in trapezoidal enclosures and associated subwoofers. The systems took advantage of the newer component technology, including Flat-Front, Bi-Radial horns, extended range compression drivers, and SFG (Symmetrical Field Geometry) cone transducers, as can be seen in the cutaway system view.

Reinforced mounting hardware integral to the enclosures permitted the arraying of systems three and four layers high, while the trapezoidal relief angles permitted arcing and rounding of the arrays for corner and end coverage. Systems were available with racks of JBL/UREI amplifiers, with signal processing and cabling. Some of the mounting variations can be seen in the photo of a permanent installation at the Concord Pavilion, Concord, CA.

Horn Loaded Array™ (HLA) Series

The HLA-Series products were designed for high level, high directionality performance in a wide variety of public entertainment applications. The individual elements are made of structural plastic and are contained within light-weight metal patented "space-frame" structures. JBL's Differential Drive transducers are used throughout the line, ensuring high output and low power compression. Both the three-way full-range 4895 module and the 4897A subwoofer module have the same main frame dimensions, facilitating the arraying of these elements.

A typical application using multiple space-frame sections is shown here. Note that in the bottom module the horn array has been tilted downward to the right. This flexibility is an advantage in making final adjustments of the array.

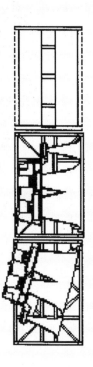

The VerTec® Family

The VerTec family was introduced in 2000 and has quickly become the array of choice in both outdoor and indoor applications. It is now available in three size classes to accommodate all requirements. Array subwoofers are also integral to this product group.

Some of the technical features of VerTec are:

Precision waveguides: For correct line array operation, very short wavelengths must radiate essentially as a continuous line, straight or curved as needed. To meet this requirement, high frequencies must be directly fed to narrow-slotted waveguides whose mouths are contiguous.

Radiation Boundary Integrator®: The midrange frequencies must radiate from a position directly adjacent to the high frequency waveguides, yet the two must not interfere with each other. The RBI accomplishes this.

Differential Drive® transducers: The midrange and low frequency drivers in the VerTec system make use of dual voice coils operating in dual neodymium magnetic gaps. This design combines the maximum output with minimum mass, making for a very light-weight overall system.

At the introduction of VerTec, JBL also presented a design program for determining the actual polar patterns in the vertical plane covered by the arrays. The response can be fine-tuned to produce uniform coverage at mid and high frequencies at the rear-most positions in large spaces. A high degree of signal coherence and uniformity of response are natural attributes of these systems.

The Grateful Dead "Wall of Sound"

In the early 1970s The Grateful Dead embarked on a new sound path. The so-called "Wall of Sound" was conceived as a set of massive vertical arrays and arc segments of cone loudspeakers, topped off with large arrays of compression driver tweeters. Each player in the band controlled his own section of the system, and the effect was one of unusually good spatiality, audio imaging and clarity. Expense was no object as banks of high-fidelity power amplifiers, piles of hookup cabling and numerous purpose-built speaker enclosures were assembled by craftsmen. But the power requirements were very high and system setup demands were intensive. Eventually, the maintenance and shipping costs mounted up, and in time, the system was retired — but not before leaving many fond memories for a generation of Dead Heads. The photo used here is courtesy of Richard Pechner. (RPechner@comcast.net)

Caljam 1974

Caljam 1974 was a signal event in the history of pop culture. On 6 April, 1974, 200,000 music fans came together at the Ontario Motor Speedway in Southern California to hear many of the best-known rock groups of the day perform, including Deep Purple and Emerson, Lake and Palmer. A sound company known as Tychobrahe (named after the early Danish astronomer) provided what was the largest sound system ever assembled at the time, supplying 54,000 watts of audio power from their custom-built amplifiers. The photo shows a view of the array at stage left. The low-frequency drivers with aluminum domes are JBL K-130s and K-140s. Rear-loaded horn enclosures are just below these, and horn-loaded subwoofers are shown positioned at the bottom. There was an identical, matching array of loudspeakers on stage right.

The US Festival and the Clair Brothers S4 System

In 1982, and again in 1983, Apple Computer co-founder Steve Wozniak sponsored huge music festival and technology expositions in Southern California. The US Festivals drew hundreds of thousands of attendees, and a huge sound system was provided by long-time JBL user Clair Brothers of Lititz, PA.

The system was composed of multiples of the Clair S4 system, first produced in 1972. This direct radiator system was approximately 4 feet square for efficient stacking and truck packing, and in its basic configuration housed two 18-inch and four 10-inch drivers, two horns and drivers, and two UHF tweeters, with the components arrayed vertically. Each side of the stage at the US Festivals had nine columns of eight-high stacked S4's for a total of 144 systems. Delay towers were provided by Showco of Dallas, TX, another long-time JBL component user. Clair Brothers' and Showco's relationships with JBL extend from the early 1960s through to the modern Showco Prism system and Clair I4 line array.

Neil Diamond, 1985

The photo shows Neil Diamond in Concert at the St. Paul, MN, Civic Center on 21 December 1985. The overhead suspended Concert Series loudspeaker arrays shown here included slightly more than 500 individual drivers in use. Stan Miller and Stanal Sound Ltd. were responsible for music reinforcement.

Presidential Inauguration, January 2001
U.S. Capitol

This 10-element VerTec line array was one of several used for the inauguration of the first term of President George W. Bush in 2001 at the United States Capitol building in Washington, D.C. The unique custom extendable support towers enabled the audio crew to locate and distribute multiple large arrays throughout a massive audience area. The pole can be extended to a height of 50 feet, starting from a footprint of only six feet square. The systems were set up in delay zones to cover the expanse of the crowd.

The rental sound system and audio support activities were provided by Maryland Sound International of Baltimore, MD. Patrick Baltzell was the event sound system designer and operator.

World Youth Day, 11 September 2005
Cologne, Germany

World Youth Day 2005, concluded with a Mass celebrated by Pope Benedict XVI for an audience estimated to be 1.1 million persons. The massive gathering required an equally immense sound system, which included 104 signal-delayed public address towers comprising JBL VerTec line array elements as the main PA for the field with hundreds of loudspeaker enclosures in use. JBL VRX series loudspeaker systems served VIP seating areas near the stage for Vatican officials and dignitaries from around the globe.

The temporary outdoor sound system, employing perhaps the largest quantity of line-array loudspeakers ever deployed at a single event, was designed and implemented by Sirius ShowEquipment AB and Crystal Sound, working in coordination with another German-based company, Neuman & Müller. The entire sound crew numbered over 85 technicians, including stagehands. Special thanks to Carsten Peter and photographer Gerd Gruss for photo images.

The German Pop Act PUR

Schalke Arena, located about 25 miles from Dusseldorf, is Germany's largest enclosed building. The massive indoor soccer arena seats 62,000 persons. The upper photo shows preparations for a concert by the German pop act PUR, carried out by Sirius ShowEquipment A.G. of Frankfurt. The bottom photo gives a good impression of the immense size of the space. Note the suspended ring of 8 VerTec loudspeaker arrays, each with 12 elements. Several nights of sold-out shows by PUR were served with this large, temporary concert audio system.

The permanent system in the Schalke Arena is also a JBL system, composed of HLA elements.

Bruce Springsteen World Tour 2002-2003

Many major international touring acts such as Bruce Springsteen travel with a complete, road-packaged concert audio system. The touring show is depicted here at the Forum in Los Angeles, CA. The photo shows four 12-element arrays of VerTec line array elements. Also facing the audience are two large VerTec subwoofer 12-element arrays. Additional side-located out-fill arrays serve the wrap-around seating, giving a full 270-degree coverage of the venue. Note also the overhead arrays facing the stage performance area for foldback monitoring. Worldwide concert sound reinforcement needs for Bruce Springsteen's tour were handled by Audio Analysts of Colorado Springs, CO.

KISS Concert Tour
Australia, 2001

The photo shows the performance stage as set up in a typical sports-venue facility for the KISS concert tour of Australia in 2001. Fifteen-element VerTec line arrays are used at left and right, with smaller outfill arrays in position for the side seating areas. Numerous subwoofer modules to support the hard-rock concert act are positioned on the deck below the front of the stage. Jands, Australia's largest and best-known concert audio service provider, supplied sound reinforcement services for the tour as well as the photo.

The 46th GRAMMY® Awards, 2004

JBL has had a special relationship with the Recording Academy for many years. As the event's annual televised awards show has grown, so has its need for sound reinforcement services, In addition, the event recently moved to a much larger facility to serve a growing live audience. VerTec line arrays are used here in the multi-purpose Staples Center in Los Angeles for the 2004 Awards Ceremonies. Scott Harmala was the sound designer, and ATK/AudioTek Corp., Valencia, CA, provided sound reinforcement services.

Democratic National Convention Boston, 2004

The October 2004 Democratic Convention was held in Boston's Fleet Center. Since the venue's permanently-installed house system was designed primarily for sporting events coverage of the seating rings, temporary large JBL VerTec line arrays were used to ensure proper speech and music coverage over the entire audience seating area, with thousands of temporary chairs in place on what would normally be the game playing floor. ATK/AudioTek Corp. of Valencia, CA. was responsible for the event audio support, and Patrick Baltzell was the sound designer for the occasion.

Republican National Convention
New York City, 2004

JBL VerTec line arrays and other systems served as the sound reinforcement platform that supported every major event of the 2004 Republican Convention, staged at Madison Square Garden. Typical of modern, large-scale political events, the program included both candidates' speeches and musical entertainment segments. The sound reinforcement system was specifically designed to support and complement the extensive broadcast audio requirements. Patrick Baltzell was the sound designer for the event, and ATK/AudioTek Corp. of Valencia, CA, provided speech and music coverage.

39th Annual Academy of Country Music Awards

The Academy of Country Music (ACM) was founded in 1964 in Los Angeles, California. It was originally called the Country & Western Music Academy, and was formed by people who wanted to share their love of country music. The event has grown to an annual, nationally-televised production to honor recording and performing artists in the musical genre. Previously held at medium sized venues, the event's popularity encouraged the Academy of Country Music to move it to the Mandalay Bay Resort & Casino Arena in Las Vegas in 2004, a much larger facility requiring the highest-quality sound system and technical production support. JBL VerTec line array systems were temporarily suspended in the 12,000 seat arena to support concert audio requirements. The 39th Academy of Country Music Awards ceremony is shown here, with sound design by Scott Harmala and audio reinforcement by ATK/AudioTek Corp., of Valencia, CA.

The Oscars, 2003
Kodak Theatre, Hollywood, CA

Since its founding in 1927, the Academy of Motion Picture Arts and Sciences has awarded Oscar statuettes for excellence in motion pictures. Beginning as an informal get-together at Hollywood's Roosevelt Hotel, today's "Oscars" are a celebrity film industry mega-event televised around the world. After many years at Los Angeles' Shrine Auditorium, the Oscars moved in 2003 to its new home, the Kodak Theatre in Hollywood. JBL's VerTec arrays are visible, left and right, in front of the proscenium. Sound reinforcement services were provided by ATK/AudioTek Corp. of Valencia, CA, and Patrick Baltzell was the sound designer. "Academy Award" and "Oscar" image ©AMPAS®.

The Oscars, 2005
Kodak Theatre, Hollywood, CA

Continuing onward at the 3,400-seat Kodak Theater, JBL has been honored to have been chosen by rental company ATK/ AudioTek, of Valencia, CA, for each Oscar occasion held in the venue, which at 120 feet wide and 75 feet deep, boasts one of the largest main stage areas in the United States. Three VerTec array locations in a left, center, right configuration are beautifully suspended over the proscenium. For 2005 Patrick Baltzell was once again the sound designer. "Academy Award" and "Oscar" image ©AMPAS®.

Tokyo Jazz Festival, 2002

Multi-act music festivals often employ temporary, portable sound system setups that are often highly complex in order to be flexible enough to serve the needs of multiple acts that will share the same stage. Here is a view of the 2002 Tokyo Jazz Festival during rehearsals and sound check. JBL VerTec line arrays with HLA subwoofer arrays positioned behind them are visible at the left and right sides of the temporary performance stage, erected in a sporting event stadium venue. An oblique view from the left shows the Festival underway, with additional arrays for side fill. Sound reinforcement was provided by TwoMix of Tokyo, and the sound designer was Kazuo Takei. Photos courtesy TwoMix.

Eric Clapton
Royal Albert Hall, London

London's Royal Albert Hall was first opened in the 1870s. In recent years it has come to host more pop and rock shows than the type of classical music events for which it was originally designed. With 6,000 seats, including numerous opera-style boxes, the venue has presented a wide range of international touring acts and special musical events. It is shown here, with three VerTec arrays, as set up for a concert by noted musician Eric Clapton, May 2004. Audio support services were provided by Concert Sound, Ltd., Luton, UK.

Radio City Music Hall
New York City

Radio City Music Hall is to New York City what the Hollywood Bowl is to Los Angeles. The auditorium seats 6000 and is used for motion pictures as well as all types of stage shows, concert performances, and seasonal events. It is shown here in the process of being setup for the annual Christmas Season series. Photo by JBL Professional.

Chapter 9: Performance Venues

Today's concert halls, both domestic and overseas, present diverse productions to a broad audience. Orchestral concerts, internationally known soloists, jazz performances, and pop acts all serve to keep the facility occupied and financially in the black. Venues can range from classically-designed structures, with acoustics that are naturally supportive of symphonic and operatic playbills, to contemporary, modernistic architectural showplaces.

The type of sound reinforcement systems required to support performances in this class of venues can vary just as much as the architectural styles represented in them. A primary challenge for sound system designers in such facilities is to anticipate what styles and types of musical and theatrical programs will be appearing on the stage in a particular building, and then tailoring the design of the building's permanent system, and its fixed facilities to accommodate different temporary sound installations in some instances, to different musical and theatrical production applications that will be encountered in that space.

For routine announcements there is normally a built-in public address system of fairly small scale. A much larger full-bandwidth system is often deployed for pop and jazz acts, as well as those rare classical performances that require high-level sound reinforcement, as may be called for in the musical score. For these purposes, system flexibility – the ease with which a 'working system' can be assembled and then taken down – is of great importance. You will notice that many of the newer venues shown here use modern line-array-type loudspeaker systems. In addition to their modular nature, these systems can be quickly adapted to changing requirements. But their major virtue may simply be that they sound very good. By its very nature as a line of closely spaced transducers, interferences between elements in systems of this type are minimized and frequency response remains quite uniform over a large uninterrupted angle of coverage.

We begin our survey with a group of legacy halls, and then move on to highlight more modern installations.

The Vienna State Opera House
Vienna, Austria

The European opera tradition has often been more in tune with modern technology than that of the United States, while at the same time, historical European venues have a strong heritage in classical acoustics with a particular 'room sound' as an inherent part of the building design. With regard to operatic productions, off-stage and extra-musical effects have, for decades, been reproduced via electroacoustical technology. The large vertical columns seen here on both sides of the Vienna State Opera House's proscenium stage opening contain a custom designed full-bandwidth system using JBL components and system elements from the HLA and Array Series. These support systems are located in the coves and are used as needed.

Royal Danish Theater
Copenhagen, Denmark

The Royal Danish Theater is typical of Europe's historic, classical performance halls. It is home to a variety of stage activities, including ballet performances, often accompanied by recorded music. A high quality stereo system is therefore a major requirement. The sound reinforcement system is housed in the large side walls of the proscenium and is normally recessed into the walls behind the grillework. The grilles are removed to reveal the 8-inch cone transducers and high frequency horns. The system is complemented by subwoofers located in the upper portions of the side walls.

JBL at the Sydney Opera House
Sydney, Australia

The Sydney Opera House is seen against the famous Harbour Bridge. This striking facility, a world-renowned architectural icon, is home to a broad range of musical and theatrical performance events. On the interior, a complex custom-designed JBL system provides reinforcement to cover the needs of various functions. The photo shows, along with the monophonic subwoofers, the center channel of a three-channel stereo complement of loudspeakers covering the front circle of the house. The mounting fixtures for the array are clearly seen in the photo, and the arrays are concealed when not in use. Component layout is shown in the drawing. HLA system elements are employed in a tapered array configuration, along with an ensemble of subwoofers. The system was designed by consultant Glenn Leembruggen and has been described in a paper in the Journal of the Audio Engineering Society. Image of the Sydney Opera House is used under license from the Sydney Opera House Trust.

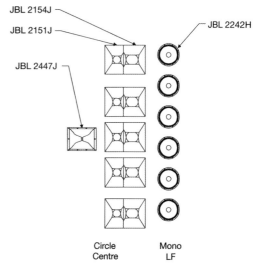

Jazz at Lincoln Center, Rose Hall
New York City

Jazz at Lincoln Center is located at the Time Warner Center at Columbus Circle in New York City. The building complex consists of Rose Hall, the main concert venue, and the Allen Room, a more intimate performance space. The complex is the home of the Jazz At Lincoln Center program headed by Pulitzer Prize-winning musician and composer, Wynton Marsalis. Mr. Marsalis also directs the Lincoln Center Jazz Orchestra, which is dedicated to developing a performance repertory of historic compositions and newly commissioned works for big band jazz ensembles.

This modern facility is representative of performance venues that must be equipped to serve a broad range of functions and events, while having a sound reinforcement system and room acoustics that are well-suited to a particular musical style. JBL VerTec line array systems and other Harman Professional components are used throughout the installation. Acoustic design of the entire facility was carried out by Artec Consultants, the Walters-Storyk Design Group, and SIA Acoustics, all of New York. Maryland Sound was responsible for the installation. Photography by Frank Stewart, JALC.

The movable rear seating towers behind the stage platform provide a unique, intimate experience for the audience and was one of the greatest electroacoustical design challenges.

Shanghai Grand Theater
Shanghai, China

The amazing skyline of Shanghai now has a stunning new performance venue for everything from opera to concerts to pop acts. Located in the northern part of the People's Square in Huangpu District, the Shanghai Grand Theater venue was designed by French architect Jean-Marie Charpentier and covers a floor area of 11,528 square meters. Loudspeakers from JBL Professional are used throughout the installation. System sub-assemblies include cove-mounted arrays, hidden subwoofers, and portable support speaker systems for deployment by the venue's audio production staff as required.

The Grand Ole Opry
Nashville, TN

The Grand Ole Opry, one of the great icons of American music culture, outgrew its traditional home at Nashville's Ryman Auditorium in the city's downtown area a number of years ago. A new, larger facility, home to regularly-scheduled broadcast radio and television shows, is equipped with all the modern devices of stagecraft. A standard 'house band' plays host to an ever-changing cast of special country music guest artists.

JBL's mid-size VerTec line array systems are used for reinforcement, with main and side arrays in position to serve the fan-shaped audience seating area and balcony. A large dedicated subwoofer array is located in the center of the loudspeaker locations. In this photo, some of the VerTec arrays can be seen as they are positioned high over the stage.

The original Ryman Auditorium and the Wild Horse Saloon Club venue are also JBL installations. Stage photo courtesy Steve Spittle.

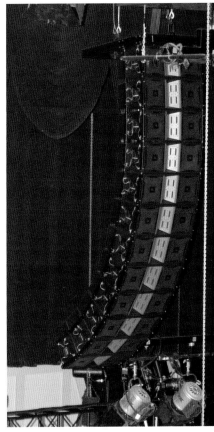

VerTec at the Greek Theater
Los Angeles, CA

With seating for 5,700 patrons, the Greek Theater is one of Los Angeles' more intimate outdoor venues. The Greek Theatre is owned by the City of Los Angeles, and is managed, operated and promoted by Nederlander-Greek Inc. This award-winning theater is one of Los Angeles' most historic entertainment venues and has played host to some of the biggest names in entertainment, from pop to classical, reggae to rock. Recent seasons have featured performances by a wide variety of artists such as The Who, Sting, Alicia Keys, Pearl Jam, Jose Carerras, Marc Anthony, Tina Turner, Elton John, Santana, The White Stripes, The Gipsy Kings, the Russian National Ballet, Paul Simon, with a special guest appearance by Sir Paul McCartney, just to name a few. This venue offers an intimate concert setting under the stars in the heart of Los Angeles. The Greek Theater won the prestigious *Best Small Outdoor Venue* award four times in its history, which was awarded by *Pollstar Magazine*, the industry's leading trade publication.

The facility relies on a seasonally-installed JBL VerTec line array system, shown here in the process of being set up by Schubert Systems Group, North Hollywood, CA, for a round of Summer performances. Left and right main loudspeaker arrays with outfill locations are augmented by special vertically-oriented subwoofer arrays, and signal-delayed compact arrays positioned at the rear of the audience seating area.

Walt Disney Concert Hall
Los Angeles, CA

The sweeping interior and exterior of architect Frank Gehry's Disney Hall are stunning to both the eyes and ears. The hall is the new home of the Los Angeles Philharmonic and has been virtually packed since its opening in 2002. The unorthodox organ case is one of a kind, but when seen within the larger context of the hall's interior, if seems to fit naturally.

JBL loudspeakers are used throughout this architecturally-innovative building for routine announcements and paging. JBL VerTec line array systems are deployed when larger-scale support is required for pop acts and other functions requiring full-bandwidth musical sound reinforcement.

The Barns at Wolf Trap
Vienna, VA

The Barns at Wolf Trap is one of the Washington, DC, area's favorite indoor performance venues for summertime entertainment. The site is actually a National Park, and "The Barns" consist of two adjacent 18th century buildings that have been converted into performance spaces. The space seats 284 patrons on the main floor and 98 in the balcony. Two sets of compact VerTec arrays are deployed on both sides of the stage.

Auditorium Parco della Musica
Rome, Italy

Noted Italian architect Renzo Piano was the designer of the Auditorium Parco della Musica in Rome. The space is somewhat reminiscent of Disney Hall in Los Angeles, both outside and in. It is a modern concert hall complex that makes extensive use of wood in its design and construction. The venue's various performance spaces are intended for multi-purpose use in addition to the support of classical music productions, and host a broad variety of concerts and special events.

The multi-hall complex includes three performance spaces with seating capacity of 2,800 (shown here), 1,200, and 700, respectively with each designed for flexibility of use for different types of productions. The 2800-seat concert hall is intended for symphony concerts, composed of a large orchestra and choir. The 1200-seat concert hall features adjustable stage and seating, according to the performance's requirements, allows a fine-tuning of the reverberation time to accommodate a large orchestra with choir, ballet, or contemporary music. The 700-seat concert hall is equipped with an orchestra pit and fly tower, similar to the configuration of a traditional theatre. A total of 88 JBL VerTec midsize and subwoofer loudspeaker enclosures are used throughout the complex.

Benaroya Hall
Seattle, WA

Built in the late 1990s, Benaroya Hall is the home of the Seattle Symphony Orchestra, and it also hosts a variety of pop and jazz performances. The acoustical design was carried out by noted consultant Cyril Harris, and the sound installation was made by CCI Solutions of Olympia, WA, under the direction of Ron Simonson.

The photo at left shows the stage set up for an orchestra rehearsal under the direction of Gerard Schwarz, Music Director of the Seattle Symphony Orchestra. The photo on this page shows the hall interior as seen from the conductor's podium. Photos courtesy CCI Solutions.

Chapter 10: Stadiums and Sports Facilities

Over the last 25 years, sports facilities, both indoors and out, have evolved into highly engineered spaces, with care given to creature comforts, improved sightlines, better sound, and, in many cases, high-ticket executive lounges found in major franchise stadiums. In the early days, sound systems were composed of individual high frequency horns and low frequency bins, all carefully adjusted to provide uniformity of coverage for given seating areas. Today, these have largely been replaced by purpose-designed system elements with specific coverage angles that can be more economically assembled via integral rigging fixtures.

Major stadiums are often located in densely populated areas, and concerns include the liability of spill of sound into neighboring residential areas. More attention is thus required at the design stage to ensure that existing civic regulations can be met.

For indoor spaces, speech clarity requires that systems project sound only where it is needed. Excessive reverberation, so detrimental to speech intelligibility, is also a major factor in listener fatigue, and systems must be capable of minimizing reverberant power, while delivering sound directly to occupied seating areas. In some cases, special systems have been developed by JBL for a given application.

In this chapter we will review the range of specific JBL hardware used in these systems, along with views of typical installations.

Precision Directivity® Products

The Precision Directivity products were developed to address problems in large enclosed sports arenas. In such spaces, sound pressures in the lower speech range from 125 Hz to 500 Hz often build up in the enclosed space due to a lack of sufficient acoustical absorption at those frequencies. In order to attain the highest possible directivity in this critical frequency range, the solution was found in multiple-woofer "forward-steered" modules. In this system, each transducer in a planar array of woofers is fired separately and timed so that the combined low frequency wave fronts all point in a predetermined direction. This enables the system to "launch," or steer, a low frequency beam as needed.

At higher frequencies, the solution was found in midrange horn systems with large mouths and a coaxially mounted high frequency section. If the two radiators are combined properly through the dividing network, the combination will provide uniform directivity from about 500 Hz upward.

More details of these techniques are presented in Chapter 2.

Application Engineered™ Products

The Application Engineered product group is a large family intended for fixed installations in performance spaces, theaters, auditoriums, houses of worship, and live music clubs. Special mid-high modules can be used without low frequency reinforcement in speech-only and delay-fill applications. The smaller models are ideal in lecture halls and corporate facilities. The mid-high front baffles can be rotated for greater flexibility in mounting and in achieving specific coverage patterns.

Array Series™

The JBL Array Series products were among the first in the industry to offer integral mounting and rigging hardware. These systems are ideal for compact touring and fixed installation, and they combine ease of transport with the flexibility for flying or installing quickly and safely. S.A.F.E. suspension hardware has been designed, engineered, and certified to meet and exceed the most stringent requirements for sound system rigging, worldwide.

As shown in the installation photo, multiple elements can be securely joined with minimal effort on the part of the installer. In the product view, the 2-way model 4892 is shown above, and the dual subwoofer model 4893 is shown below.

Control® Contractor Series

Designed as an extension of the original Control 1 and Control 5 molded multi-purpose utility loudspeaker systems introduced in the mid-1980s, the Control Contractor Series was specifically developed for use in permanent installations by sound contractors in restaurants, retail, boardrooms, transportation terminals and other commercial applications. There are several product groups, all making use of attractive modern design and, where applicable, rugged molded enclosures. Surface Mount models are normally positioned on walls using the patented Invisiball® mounting bracket. Ceiling Mount models, and In-Wall models are used where a flush-mount is desirable. For larger installations, two-way and three-way surface mount products can be specified for multichannel music, including subwoofer modules.

Such applications as we have described here are essential for paging and background music applications that take place "behind the scenes" in virtually all modern sports facilities.

Surface Mount Loudspeaker

Ceiling Flush-Mount Loudspeaker

In-Wall Loudspeaker

Key Arena
Seattle, WA

Key Arena is the home of the Seattle Supersonics. The main JBL array is positioned over and around the central scoreboard, and the system, designed by Seattle Center's Richard Erwin, consists of four large arrays augmented by smaller arrays. JBL Precision Directivity models PD100 and PD700 are used. Data courtesy Ron Simonson and CCI Systems.

The low frequency solution is an example of a forward steered array. The low frequency arrays can be seen in the center of the large arrays. This installation was part of a large expansion refit and upgrade of the original Seattle Center Arena.

St. James' Park
Newcastle, UK

St. James' Park is the home of Premier League football team Newcastle United. The Park is one of the largest stadiums in Europe, and the sound system was a collaboration between Romers' John Caton and JBL's UK personnel.

As seen in the upper photo, loudspeakers are positioned in the vast overhead canopy in both an outer ring, which serves the upper seating areas, and an inner ring at the edge of the canopy, which serves the lower seating areas. Model PD5000 modules are used in this installation. Romers was established in 1925, making it one of the longest-lived institutions in all of audio. Photos courtesy of John Caton.

The Bell Centre
Montreal, QU

The Bell Centre, formerly known as the Molson Centre, has been the home of the Montreal Canadiens hockey team since 1996. The name was changed to Centre Bell in September 2002, when Bell Canada acquired the naming rights. Located in downtown Montreal, it is popular not only for hockey but also for a variety of pop acts. With seating in excess of 21,000, the space is considerably larger than most sports arenas.

The JBL system is located in the central scoreboard structure, with auxiliary under-balcony loudspeakers in the periphery. Special thanks to Jean Daoust and to the Bell Centre.

Safeco Field
Seattle, WA

The beginnings of Safeco Field date to 1995, when both county and state developed a plan for financing a new state-of-the-art stadium. What eventually came to pass in 1999 was a stadium with one of the most unusual retractable roof structures in modern stadium history. It is composed of a number of nesting sections which slide beneath one another when the roof is retracted. The final rounded section then rotates so that it exposes the maximum amount of skylight possible over the playing field and the 47,000 seats. Naming rights were secured by Safeco, a Seattle-based insurance and investment company. Custom JBL distributed systems are used in this installation.

The sound system was designed and installed by CCI Solutions, Olympia, WA.

Soldier Field
Chicago, IL

The JBL system at Soldier Field consists of VerTec and Precision Directivity components placed at the back of the top tier of seating, as seen in the upper photo. These elements are aimed at the opposing seating areas some 200 feet away. The photo at upper right shows details of one of these clusters. You can see that these systems are meant to last a long time and put up with Chicago's fierce winter weather. The shadowed areas under the various seating levels are outfitted with their own fill loudspeakers as needed. Photos courtesy Bernard Werner.

This design was based on a concept by Jack Wrightson (WJHW) in collaboration with JBL's Brad Ricks combining a long-throw line array system for one side of the stadium with a large distributed system for the near side. This was required by the unique architectural challenges presented by the refit of this historic U.S. landmark stadium. The loudspeaker clusters are the highest point in the stadium, with the center array requiring an FAA warning beacon affixed.

University of Carabobo
Venezuela

The State University of Carabobo is not far from Caracas, the Capital of Venezuela. In keeping with the tropical climate, the new Sports Complex at the University has a permanent tent structure, open on all sides to provide year-round ventilation. Numerous JBL Control Contractor 30 loudspeakers (shown in circles) provide sound coverage for both sports and entertainment events. Special thanks to Preben Jeppersen.

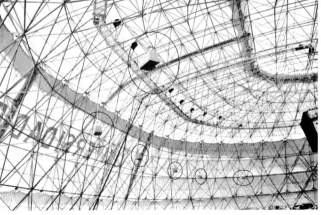

Monster Park
San Francisco, CA

In 2004, the historical home of the San Francisco 49ers was officially changed from 3COM Park to Monster Park. The naming rights were acquired by Monster Cable, one of the world's largest producers of audio cable. Not since the renaming of Philharmonic Hall in New York as Avery Fisher Hall has an audio company attained – or bought – such acclaim. The seating capacity of Monster Park is right at 70,000. JBL's Ted Leamy worked with Pro Media/UltraSound personnel to come up with a combination of Precision Directivity and Application Engineered systems to cover all aspects of sound reinforcement. Special thanks to Drew Serb.

The Oakland Arena
Oakland, CA

The Oakland Arena was constructed in 1966. Over the years, as the area became increasingly outdated, there was talk of razing it and building a new arena. A compromise was reached, and by 1996 a decision to make substantial renovations to the present structure was made, leaving the external walls, foundation and roof intact, while building an all-new interior and bowl.

Home of the Golden State Warriors since 1966, the Oakland Arena has a giant JBL system located on a ring directly above the center scoreboard. Composed of custom JBL loudspeakers utilizing large format waveguides, the system provides coverage for the main seating bowl. The boxes and suites are covered by their own local systems. Data courtesy Drew Serb and Pro Media/UltraSound.

American Airlines Center
Dallas, TX

The upper photo shows a section of JBL Precision Directivity components in the American Airlines Center in Dallas, TX. The lower illustration shows details of the array. Both low frequency and mid-high frequency components are used reinforce speech and music with high power and clarity over the entire space. Consultants were Wrightson, Johnson, Haddon & Williams, of Dallas, TX, and the installers were Pro Media/UltraSound. Special thanks to Drew Serb.

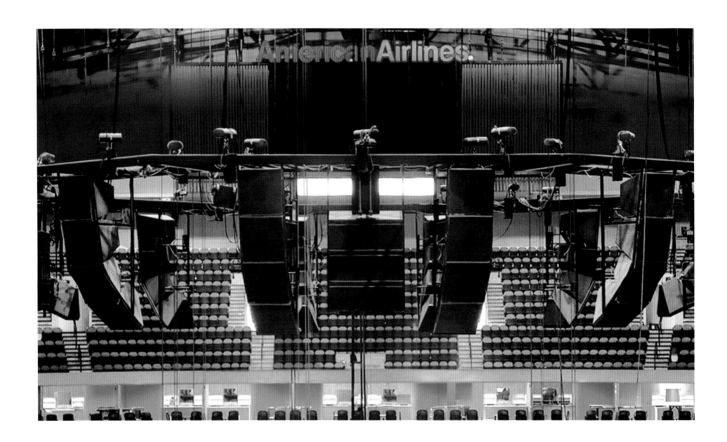

Shanghai Stadium

Speaking of naming rights – during the first few years of its operation, Shanghai Stadium honored JBL by putting its logo into the seating area! The stadium is used not only for sports functions; cultural and folk events, such as those shown in the photograph, are very popular in China as well. The stadium seats 80,000 patrons for most functions, but this is cut down to 65,000 seats for soccer games.

Structurally, a large curved canopy surrounds the periphery of the seating bowl, providing shade and shelter from the sun and various elements. This structure also provides an ideal position for mounting loudspeakers for uniform coverage of the entire seating area.

Globe Arena
Stockholm, Sweden

The Globe Arena is the largest spherical stadium in the world, measuring 110 meters in diameter. The major acoustical problem was dealing with the complex reflection patterns. Large absorbers were placed just above the center of the space to attenuate focused sound passing through that region. In addition the upper half of the sphere was covered with 100-mm thick mineral wool positioned 2 meters from the outer shell. The loudspeaker array is shown here lowered for service below the video screens. In normal operation it is positioned above the video screens. The custom JBL array was designed by Henrik Staffeldt and Per Kolding.

Chapter 11: Clubs, Business, and Commercial Systems

An important area in recent growth for JBL Professional is systems intended for places of business, such as retail stores, restaurants, transportation terminals, museums, and the like. Also included here are clubs and discotheques.

The nature of business and transportation installations is that there may be many zones, completely independent of one another, and many of which may be stand-alone. Advanced signal processing is necessary for level adjustment and program re-equalization, depending on local ambient noise. In recent years, business systems have taken on the responsibilities of voice warning in case of emergencies, including urgent evacuation announcements to patrons.

Because sound system installations are ordinarily a part of a much larger building budget, bidding for both equipment and installation is likely to be quite competitive. Both performance and unit costs are important, and in most cases the deciding factor in vendor selection will be an assessment of performance-per-dollar. The competitive edge often goes to the company that provides better performance, even though the cost may be slightly higher.

The world of dance music and disco has always looked to JBL for the best componentry available, and it would be difficult to estimate the total number of high frequency JBL ring radiators that are to be found in discos worldwide today. In recent years the line array has taken over this market, as you will see in these pages.

The Fossil Store in Woodland Mall Grand Rapids, MI

Fossil was founded in 1984. It is known primarily for its unique watch collection along with other personal accessories and items of clothing, largely of leather. Current annual sales are estimated at $850 million through both stores and e-commerce. Fossil Stores are found in upscale shopping centers across the international scene, as well as in dedicated sales areas in upscale department stores. The name derives from the company's predilection for exotic and ethnic sources.

For Fossil, a sound system is more than a conveyor of background music and an occasional page. It can set an appropriate mood, varied during the business day as required. The system in this store, a multiple satellite-with-subwoofer, was installed by Pro-Motion of Wixom, MI, using only the highest quality JBL Control Contractor products. Thanks to Lynn Matson of Pro-Motion for permission to use this photo.

EMP (Experience Music Project)
Seattle, WA

Seattle's EMP is many things, including among other features a Music Museum, a Learning Lab, a Sound Lab, a Science Fiction Museum and Hall of Fame, The Hendrix Gallery (a tribute to the late Jimi Hendrix), and the JBL Theatre. The architect was Frank Gehry, whose great success, the Walt Disney Concert Hall in Los Angeles, was patterned after EMP. The JBL equipment list includes a wide variety of items from Control Contractor Series to VerTec line arrays.

The Cheesecake Factory Restaurants

Cheesecake Factory, Incorporated, is one of the largest restaurant companies in the United States and operates about 108 upscale, casual restaurants. The company dates from 1978 and has grown substantially from those early days when it operated a "test restaurant" for dessert items made in its own bakery. Over the years, that restaurant grew in its own right and established a reputation for eclectic offerings, big California-style proportions — and of course cheesecake. The company went public in 1992.

All of the Cheesecake Factory restaurants in the United States use JBL loudspeakers for background music and occasional paging. The models include flush-mounted ceiling speakers as well as larger Control Contractor units for music reproduction. The owner of the restaurant shown here is a drummer, for whom high-quality audio is an essential design element that contributes to the customer's overall satisfaction.

The Alex Bistro
Berlin, Germany

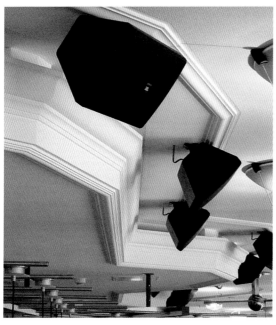

The Alex Bistros are all modern with a slight retro touch in the architectural details. Never have you seen such a dense array of JBL Control Contractor loudspeakers in a restaurant! Obviously, someone here has an ear for good sound reproduction and wants to ensure that everyone can hear well.

The Alex Bistro chain has many branches in Germany, and shown here is an installation in a Berlin location consisting of JBL Control Contractor models throughout. The installation was by Teuber-Tontechnik, Bleifeld, Germany. Photos courtesy Willi Teuber.

The Capitale Club and Restaurant
New York City

Capitale is one of New York's most exciting "event spaces," and was built on the site of the old Bowery Savings Bank (1893). The Grand Venetian Ballroom has Corinthian columns 75 feet tall and can seat 700 guests for banquets, or 2000 for standing functions. On the same premises is the Capitale Restaurant and two executive meeting areas. The Capitale is in great demand for private functions, including receptions, anniversaries, and a variety of corporate events.

One would hardly think that VerTec arrays and Applications Engineered subwoofers, both with their high-tech look and bright lighting, would fit into the main ballroom in such a complementary manner, as shown here. Special thanks to Sam Yee and to Sam Helms of Sigmet Corporation.

The Copacabana Nightclub
New York City

The open loft-like ceiling treatment contrasts nicely with the spotless, satin sheen of the dance floor. Custom JBL loudspeakers are used in this installation. Special thanks to Kevin Zambrana and to Sam Helms of Sigmet Corporation.

The Roxy Nightclub
New York City

The Roxy Nightclub uses overhead VerTec modules and floor-level subwoofers to generate high levels of clean sound at very low levels of distortion. The décor is high-tech modern – such as you might find in a New York loft – but with great splashes of inviting color. Special thanks to Steve Dash and to Sam Helms of Sigmet Corporation.

Mucho Teatro
El Puerto de Santa Maria, Spain

Located on the Bay of Cadiz on the southern tip of Spain, Mucho Teatro was once a cinema. In 2003 it was developed into a nightclub, and shown here is the main dance area on the ground floor. Theater boxes, bars, and private meeting areas are available on the first and second floors. Eight VerTec 4888 units cover the main dance floor, and the cabaret-style stage uses EON systems. Alvaro Linares was responsible for décor, and the installation was made by RIVAS SONIDO. Project consultant was EARPRO S. A. Special thanks to Martin Seidl.

Oceana Nightclub
Kingston-on-Thames, UK

Opulence and elegance go together in this installation by the Over Audio company of Bootle, Merseyside, UK. The club has seven main rooms, each following a different design motif, and a multitude of bars. JBL components range from small Control Contractor models to high-level systems covering the dance floors in the Vienna Ballroom and the Disco New York spaces.

The Bora-Bora Nui Resort and Spa

Bora-Bora is a small South Pacific island in French Polynesia, and the Bora-Bora Nui Resort and Spa, with its 120 suites and villas, conveys the image of both luxury and informal island living. JBL Control Contractor loudspeakers are used throughout the complex for paging and background music. Loudspeakers located in humid, open-air locations are subject to abuse from the environment. Using Control Contractor models with stainless steel grilles ensures reliability and longevity in such locations.

Photos courtesy the Starwood Group and Total Video Distribution.

Chapter 12: Systems for Houses of Worship

Churches, synagogues, mosques, and temples must communicate the spoken word, and in the modern era the primary function of a sound system is to enable all members of the congregation to clearly understand the verbal message. Traditionally, choral and liturgical music needed no additional sound reinforcement. Likewise, pipe organs needed no reinforcement, but electronic instruments relied on their own self-contained audio systems.

The introduction of modern evangelical worship styles has changed all of this. Many new churches are quite large and require extensive sound systems to accompany congregational singing — as well as amplify the modern pop-type instrumental ensembles that are now very common. It is also common to find extensive video recording activities and large-screen projection systems in modern houses of worship, as every attempt is made to immerse congregants in all aspects of the worship service.

In this chapter we will show JBL installations, dating from the LDS Mormon Tabernacle in Salt Lake City, UT, in the 1960s to the newest mega-churches of today.

The Mormon Tabernacle, Early 1960s
Salt Lake City, UT

The Mormon Tabernacle, home of the world-renowned choir of the same name, is an historic structure located in Salt Lake City's downtown area. This early professional installation photo shows the JBL system used in the Tabernacle to amplify the organ, via recordings, during the regular tours given in the Tabernacle. The system consisted of 15-inch woofers and high frequency horn/lens combinations, and was self-amplified with JBL Energizer modules installed in the rear of the enclosures. Today, the organ "plays itself" by way of a MIDI-controlled digital playback system that can be engaged for tour demonstrations at any time.

Domed Church in Alterlaa, Austria

Alterlaa, a suburb of Vienna, is the site of this modern Catholic Church, with an overhead ceiling dome providing natural light that suffuses the entire space. A ring of JBL Control 1 loudspeakers, installed in 1985, follows the outline of the base of the dome and provides uniform speech coverage of the seating area. This is an example of just how clean and simple a speech-only reinforcement system can be in a small worship venue.

Shrine Church of Saint Stanislaus
Cleveland, OH

This beautifully ornate church speaks to an earlier era in the history of American church-building. This particular space is highly reverberant, and the use of column arrays on each pier provides a high direct-to-reverberant ratio for speech signals intended to be heard at all seating positions throughout the church. The JBL systems can be seen positioned on each pier at a height of about 10 feet (3 meters). Sequential delaying of the audio signals from front to rear in the nave results in a greater sense of natural sound. Installation by Sound Com Corporation, Berea, OH. Special thanks to Brendan Dillon.

The Mariners Church
Irvine, CA

The Mariners Church of Irvine, CA is located in a modern structure with 3,200 seats. This church's mission is one of world outreach, and its worship style is clearly contemporary. As can be seen from the photo, overhead trusswork supports theater-style lighting facilities and JBL VerTec line array loudspeakers. A wide variety of musical types may be heard in this facility, and large-scale video projection keeps the congregation connected to events taking place on the main platform. Acoustic Dimensions provided consulting guidance in areas of acoustics and visual aspects. CCI Solutions of Olympia, WA, provided the sound system.

The City Church, Sammamish Campus
Sammamish, WA

The City Church in Sammamish, WA, combines a traditional architectural style with a robust, full-bandwidth sound system more characteristic of contemporary worship spaces. Employing two main arrays, the stereo system consists of twelve JBL VerTec midsize VT4888 units and a pair of down-fill elements. The sound system was designed and installed by Morgan Sound of Seattle, a JBL dealer for more than 30 years. Steve Gregory was the project leader. Photo courtesy of Charles Morgan.

Church of the Servant
Oklahoma City, OK

The present home of the United Methodist Church of the Servant was dedicated in 1993. The building is pyramidal in overall shape, and the main worship area is rectangular with the pulpit at one end and all musical resources (choir and orchestra) at the other end. There are two loudspeaker arrays located left and right above the pulpit, with an identical pair at the rear for choir and orchestra reinforcement. All four arrays are mounted behind scrim and are designed around JBL 2350-Series horns. There are side-fill distributed loudspeakers that are time-zoned separately for each array pair. Thus, when the Pastor is speaking, the sequential delays are from east to west; when music is performed, the sequential delays are from west to east. Both systems can operate independently of each other – or in concert with each other.

The complex reinforcement systems was designed and installed by Ford Audio-Video of Oklahoma City, and the building architect was Bill Howard & Associates. Additional JBL installations were installed by Ford Audio-Video in the Fellowship Hall, Chapel, and Youth Center. Special thanks to Jim Ford.

The Christian Church at Brunstad
International Conference Center
Oslo, Norway

The Christian Church rents space at the Brunstad International Congress Center near Oslo for its worship services. The multi-purpose space can accommodate 7,500 persons, and, in addition to worship services, plays host to a wide range of civic, business and entertainment meetings and activities. The extensive JBL system, installed by LydRommet, includes 32 mid-size VerTec line array elements, 8 compact VerTec units, and 6 VerTec subwoofers. Shown here, the facility's grand opening show and ceremony staged in July, 2004 with extensive multi-media production elements.

The Lakewood Church
Houston, TX

The Lakewood Church in Houston, TX, is one of the largest worship structures in the world. It was formerly Summit Basketball Stadium, and in 2005, after extensive remodeling, was reopened as Lakewood Church. Pastor Joel Osteen and his in-house audio staff chose Audio Analysts, of Colorado Springs, CO, with whom he had worked on previous touring occasions, as the best company to tackle the audio problems inherent in such a large space. According to Albert Leccese, Vice-President of Engineering for Audio Analysts, "The sound needed to come across as being very, very live. We needed 50 voices to sound like a huge choir, and for the spoken word to sound crisp and clear at every seat in the massive venue." Both reverberation time and noise, which are difficult problems in such large spaces, were reduced to acceptable levels through the thoughtful application of JBL's VerTec line array technology, and all 16,000 worshipers are reportedly able to hear without difficulty. Photos courtesy Steve Johnson, HP Marketing Company.

Chapter 13: JBL Transducer Timelines

The timeline charts presented here are based on original tabulations generated by Stereo Sound in Japan. The original charts were published in 1996, and we have extended them to 2006. Special thanks to Koji Onodera, Editor of Stereo Sound, for permission to use their original data.

These charts outline the development of JBL transducers over a 60 year period. In the early days of the company, transducers were sales models that were in all consumer catalogs. By the middle 1970s the Consumer group removed transducers from the catalog as they focused on the sales of complete systems. By comparison, the Professional catalog continued its sales of individual transducers as components to be used in the design of complete systems for the end user.

In every case, Pro transducers are documented as to their dates of introduction and dates of discontinuance, or replacement by a running model change. Regarding the recent history of Consumer product development, many new transducers have been developed that are specific to a particular product group, and as such may not be listed here. Exceptions here are the transducers developed for the various Consumer flagship models for the Japanese market.

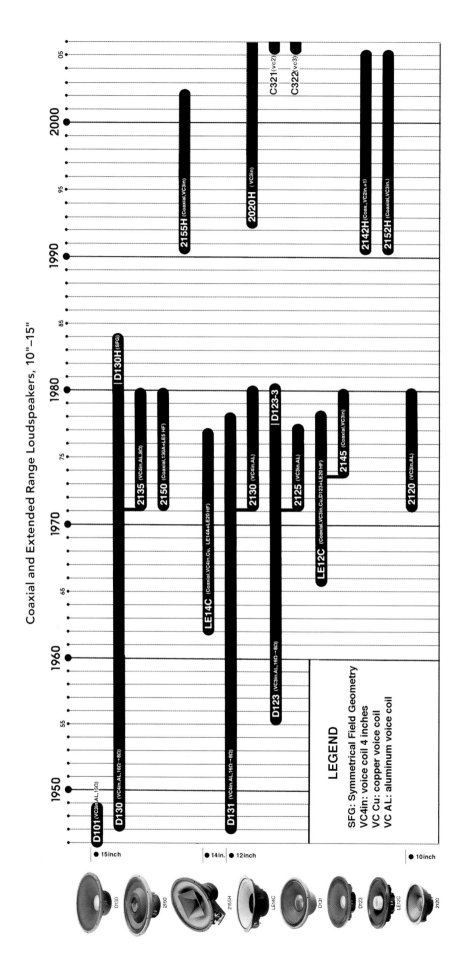

Coaxial and Extended Range Loudspeakers, 10"–15"

LEGEND

SFG: Symmetrical Field Geometry
VC4in: voice coil 4 inches
VC Cu: copper voice coil
VC AL: aluminum voice coil

5"–8" Extended Range/Speach Range; Musical Instrument

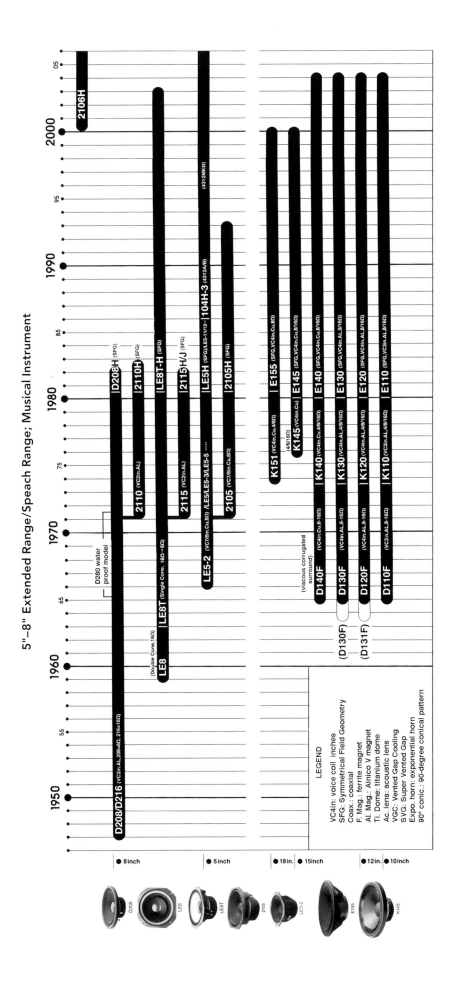

LEGEND

VC4in: voice coil inches
SFG: Symmetrical Field Geometry
Coax.: coaxial
F. Mag.: ferrite magnet
Al. Mag.: Alnico V magnet
Ti. Dome: titanium dome
Ac. lens: acoustic lens
VGC: Vented Gap Cooling
SVG: Super Vented Gap
Expo. horn: exponential horn
90° conic.: 90-degree conical pattern

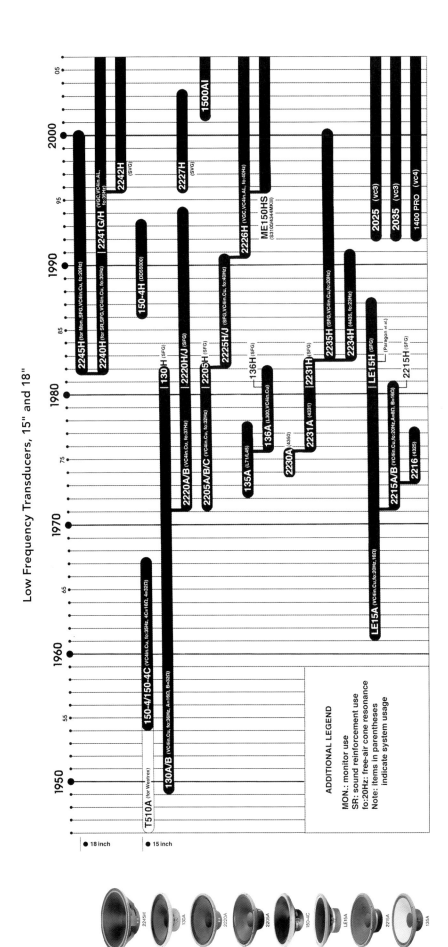

Low Frequency Transducers, 15" and 18"

ADDITIONAL LEGEND

MON.: monitor use
SR: sound reinforcement use
fo:20Hz: free-air cone resonance
Note: items in parentheses
indicate system usage

● 18 inch   ● 15 inch

Low Frequency Transducers, 12"–14"

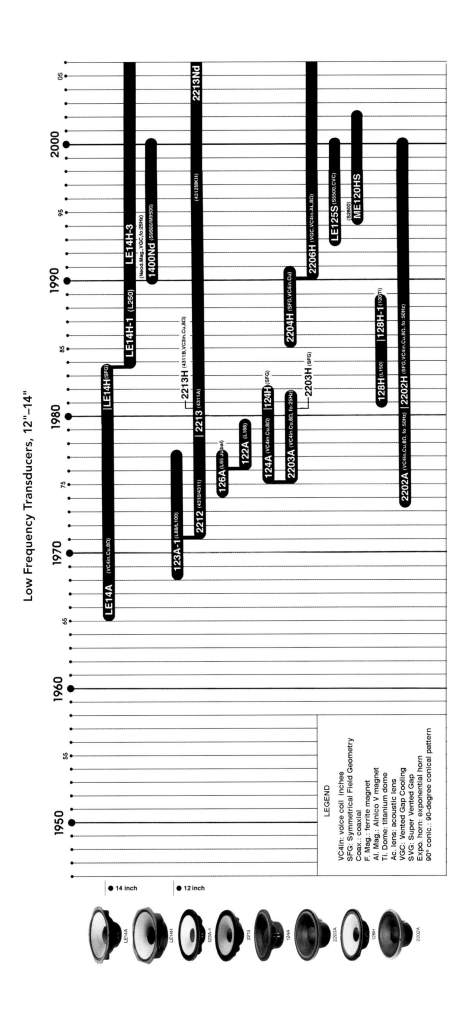

LEGEND

VC4in: voice coil inches
SFG: Symmetrical Field Geometry
Coax.: coaxial
F. Mag.: ferrite magnet
Al. Mag.: Alnico V magnet
Ti. Dome: titanium dome
Ac. lens: acoustic lens
VGC: Vented Gap Cooling
SVG: Super Vented Gap
Expo. horn: exponential horn
90° conic.: 90-degree conical pattern

● 14 inch   ● 12 inch

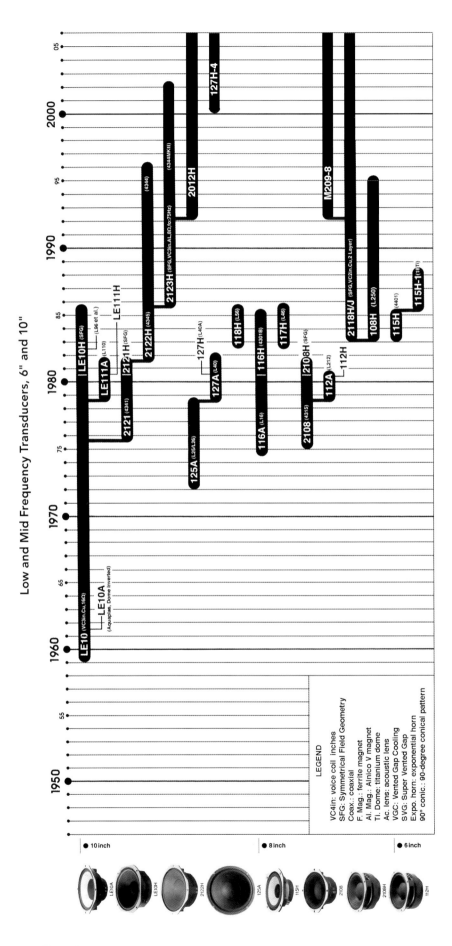

Low and Mid Frequency Transducers, 6" and 10"

LEGEND

VC4in: voice coil inches
SFG: Symmetrical Field Geometry
Coax.: coaxial
F. Mag.: ferrite magnet
Al. Mag.: Alnico V magnet
Ti. Dome: titanium dome
Ac. lens: acoustic lens
VGC: Vented Gap Cooling
SVG: Super Vented Gap
Expo. horn: exponential horn
90° conic.: 90-degree conical pattern

● 10 inch

● 8 inch

● 6 inch

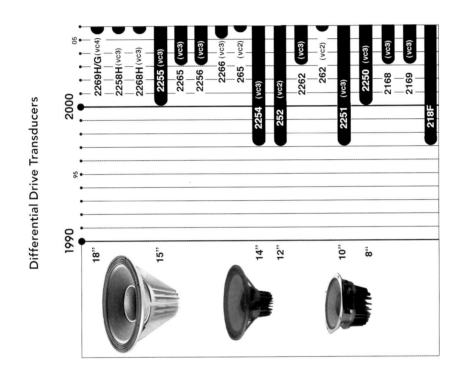

Differential Drive Transducers

1990   95   2000   05

18"
15"
14"
12"
10"
8"

2269H/G (vc4)
2258H (vc3)
2268H (vc3)
2255 (vc3)
2265 (vc3)
2256 (vc3)
2266 (vc3)
265 (vc2)
2254 (vc3)
252 (vc2)
2262 (vc3)
262 (vc2)
2251 (vc3)
2250 (vc3)
2168 (vc3)
2169 (vc3)
218F

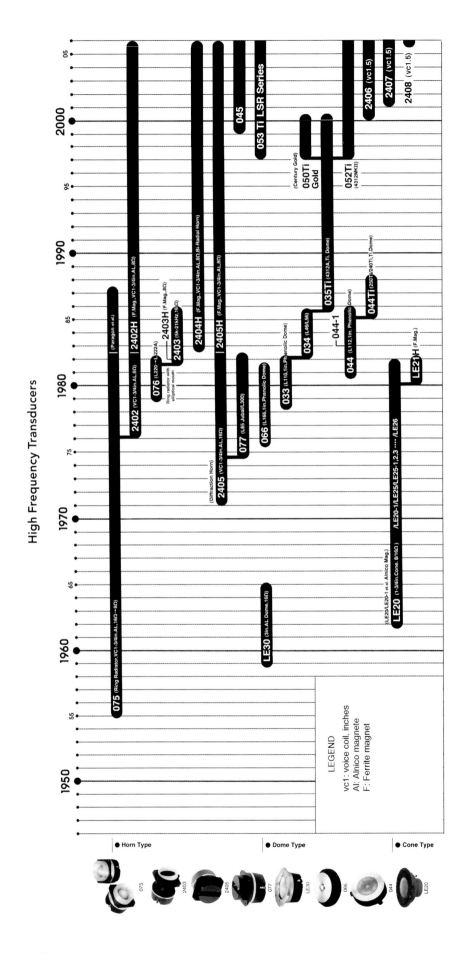

High Frequency Transducers

LEGEND
vc1 : voice coil, inches
Al: Alnico magnete
F: Ferrite magnet

● Horn Type   ● Dome Type   ● Cone Type

1950 55 1960 65 1970 75 1980 85 1990 95 2000 05

075 (Ring Radiator,VC1-3/4in.AL,16Ω→8Ω)

2402 (VC1-3/4in.AL,8Ω)

2402H (F-Mag.,VC1-3/4in.AL,8Ω)

(Paragon et al.)

076 (L220→L222A)

2403 (5k-21kHz,16Ω)

2403H (F-Mag.,8Ω)

2404H (F-Mag.,VC1-3/4in.AL,8Ω,Bi-Radial Horn)

2405 (VC1-3/4in.AL,16Ω)

(Diffraction Horn)

2405H (F-Mag.,VC1-3/4in.AL,8Ω)

077 (L65-Jubal/L300)

066 (L166,1in.Phenolic Dome)

033 (L110,1in.Phenolic Dome)

034 (L46/L56)

044-1

044 (L112,1in. Phenolic Dome)

035Ti (4312A,Ti. Dome)

044Ti (250Ti/240Ti,T. Dome)

045

053 Ti LSR Series

(Century Gold)
050Ti
Gold

052Ti
(4312MKII)

LE30 (3in.AL.Dome,16Ω)

LE20 (1-3/4in.Cone, 8/16Ω)

(LE20/LE20-1 et al. Alnico Mag.)

/LE20-1/LE25/LE25-1,2,3 ···· /LE26

LE21H (F-Mag.)

2406 (vc1.5)

2407 (vc1.5)

2408 (vc1.5)

075

2403

2405

077

LE30

066

044

LE20

Compression Drivers

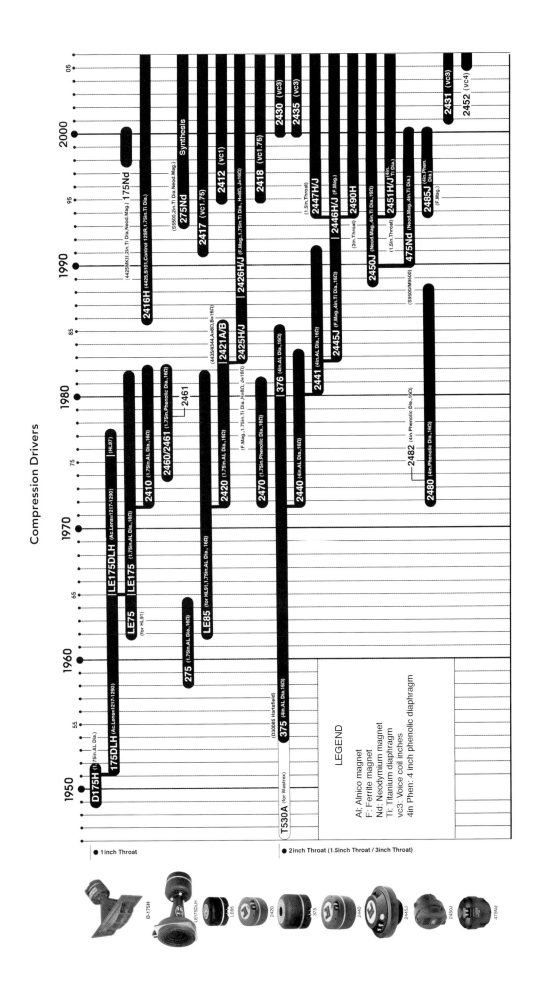

Horn-lens Assemblies, 2"–3" Throats

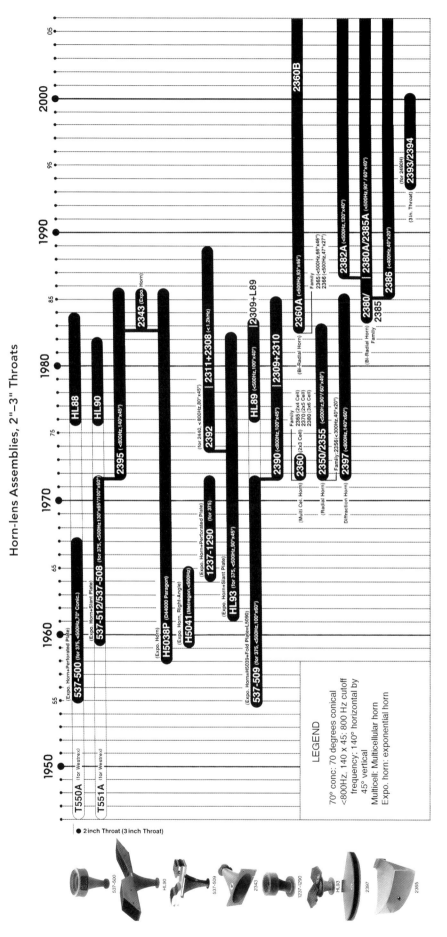

Timeline axis (left to right): 1950, 55, 1960, 65, 1970, 75, 1980, 85, 1990, 95, 2000, 05

- T550A (for Westrex)
- T551A (for Westrex)
- (Expo. Horn+Perforated Plate) **537-500** (for 375, <500Hz, 70° Conic.)
- (Expo. Horn+Slant Plate) **537-512/537-508** (for 375, <500Hz,130°x65°/100°x60°)
- (Expo. Horn) **H5038P** (D40000 Paragon)
- (Expo. Horn, Right-Angle) **H5041** (Metregon, <500Hz)
- **2395** (<800Hz,140°x45°)
- **2343** (Expo. Horn)
- (Expo. Horn+Perforated Plate) **1237-1290** (for 375)
- **2392** (for 2440, <800Hz,80°x45°)
- **2311+2308** (<1.2kHz)
- (Expo. Horn+Slant Plate) **HL93** (for 375, <500Hz,90°x45°)
- (Expo. Horn=H5039+Fold Plate=L5090) **537-509** (for 375, <500Hz,100°x60°)
- **HL88**
- **HL90**
- **HL89** (<500Hz,100°x45°)
- **2309+2310**
- **2309+L89**
- **2390** (<800Hz,100°x45°)
- (Multi Cel. Horn) **2360** (2x3 Cell) — Family 2365 (2x4 Cell) 2370 (2x5 Cell) 2380 (3x6 Cell)
- (Radial Horn) **2350/2355** (<500Hz,90°/60°x40°)
- (Diffraction Horn) **2397** (<800Hz,140°x60°) — Family 2356 (<300Hz,40°x20°)
- (Bi-Radial Horn) **2360A** (<500Hz,93°x46°) — Family 2365 (<500Hz,66°x46°) 2366 (<500Hz,47°x27°)
- **2360B**
- **2382A** (<800Hz,120°x40°)
- (Bi-Radial Horn) **2380/2385A** (<500Hz,90°/60°x40°) — Family
- **2380/2385**
- **2386** (<400Hz,40°x20°)
- (3in. Throat) **2393/2394** (for 2490H)

LEGEND

70° conc: 70 degrees conical
<800Hz, 140 x 45: 800 Hz cutoff
  frequency; 140° horizontal by
  45° vertical
Multicell: Multicellular horn
Expo. horn: exponential horn

● 2 inch Throat (3 inch Throat)

Component photos (left to right): 537-500, HL90, 537-509, 2343, 1237-1290, HL93, 2397, 2355

Horns and lenses, 1"–1.5" Throats

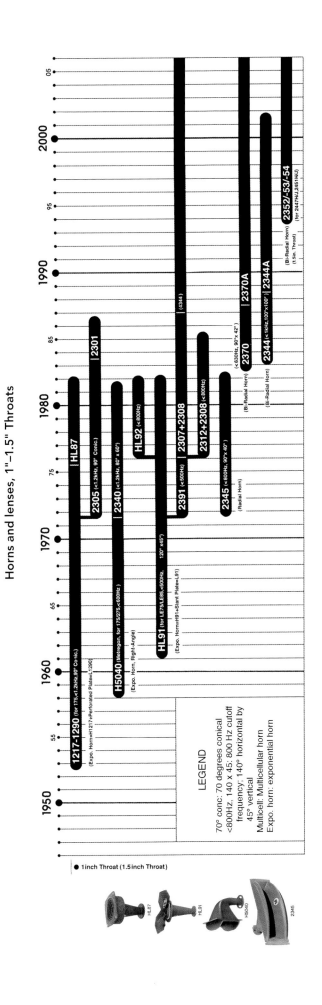

1217-1290 (for 175/<1.2kHz,90° Conic.)
(Expo. Horn=H1217+Perforated Plate=L1290)

H5040 (Metragon, for 175/275,<600Hz)
(Expo. Horn, Right-Angle)

HL87
2305 (<1.2kHz,90° Conic.)
2340 (<1.2kHz, 80° x 60°)

HL92 (<800Hz)
HL91 (for LE75/LE85,<600Hz,
120° x45°)
(Expo. Horn=H91+Slant Plate=L91)

2391 (<500Hz)
2307+2308

2312+2308 (<800Hz)

2301

(4344)

2345 (<800Hz, 90°x40°)
(Radial Horn)

2370 (<800Hz, 90°x 42°)
2370A
(Bi-Radial Horn)

2344 (<1kHz,100°x100°) **2344A**
(Bi-Radial Horn)

2352/-53/-54
(Bi-Radial Horn)
(1.5in. Throat)   (for 2447H/J,2451H/J)

LEGEND
70° conc: 70 degrees conical
<800Hz, 140 x 45: 800 Hz cutoff
frequency; 140° horizontal by
45° vertical
Multicell: Multicellular horn
Expo. horn: exponential horn

● 1inch Throat (1.5inch Throat)

HL87   HL91   H5040   2345

Chapter 14: Technical Writings and Patents

Section I: Technical Papers and Books Written by JBL Staff Members

The items listed here exist as published material in relevant journals, magazines, proceedings, and books to be found in most technical libraries. A large portion of them exist in electronic form and may be downloaded via the Internet. In general, they were written by persons who were associated with JBL at the time the article was published or in preparation. A particular exception is made here in the inclusion of several papers by James B. Lansing written during his Altec Lansing years.

George Augspurger:

"Horn-type Speaker Systems,"
Radio Electronics, May 1955

"Double Chamber Speaker Enclosure,"
Electronics World, December 1961

"The Importance of Loudspeaker Efficiency,"
Electronics World, January 1962

"The Acoustic Lens," Electronics
World, December 1962

"The Magnet: Heart of the Loudspeaker,"
Hi-Fi Stereo Review, August 1965

"The Damping Factor Debate," Electronics
World, January 1967

"Direct vs. Reverberant Sound for Stereo
Speakers," Electronics World, 1970

Sound Workshop Manual, JBL Publication,
1977; (sections reprinted in J. Eargle
"Sound System Design Reference Manual,"
1982, 1986, and 1999, JBL Professional)

David Bie:

"Vibration Resonances of a Titanium
Loudspeaker Diaphragm." Preprint
4642, AES Convention 104 (1998)

"Normal Modes of Some Common Thin Metal
Diaphragms," Preprint 2982, AES Convention
89 (1990)

"Design and Theory of a New Midrange Horn
Driver," Preprint 3429, AES Convention
93 (1992)

Douglas Button:

"A Loudspeaker Motor Structure for Very High
Power Handling and High Linear Excursion,"
JAES volume 36, number 10 (September 1988)
Also Preprint 2553, AES Convention 83 (1987)

"Heat Dissipation and Power Compression
in Loudspeakers," JAES volume 40,
number 1/2 (December 1991) Also Preprint
2981, AES Convention 89 (1990)

"Design Parameters and Trade-Offs in
Large Diameter Transducers," Preprint
3192, AES Convention 91 (1991)

"Maximum SPL from Direct Radiators," Preprint
3934, AES Convention 97 (October 1994)

"Magnetic Circuit Design Methodologies for Dual-Coil Transducers," JAES volume 50, number 6 (May 2002) Also Preprint 4622, AES Convention 103 (1997)

"The Dual-Coil Drive Loudspeaker," Paper MAL-14, AES UK Conference on Microphones and Loudspeakers: The Ins and Outs of Audio (MAL, February 1998); co-author Mark Gander

"Maximizing Performance from Loudspeaker Ports," JAES volume 50, number 1 (December 2001); co-authors: Alex Salvatti and Alan Devantier. Also Preprint 4855, AES Convention 105 (1998)

"High Frequency Components for High Output Articulated Line Arrays," Preprint 5684, AES Convention 113 (September 2002)

"Ground Plane Constant Beam Width Transducer (CBT) Loudspeaker Circular-Arc Arrays," Preprint 6594, AES Convention 119 (2005); co-author: D. B. Keele

Alan Devantier:

"Maximizing Performance from Loudspeaker Ports," JAES volume 50, number 1 (December 2001); co-authors: Alex Salvatti and Douglas Button. Also Preprint 4855, AES Convention 105 (1998)

"Characterizing the Amplitude Response of Loudspeaker Systems," Preprint 5638, AES Convention 113 (2002)

"In-Room Low Frequency Optimization," Preprint 5942, AES Convention 115 (2003); co-author: T. Welti

"Analysis and Modeling of the bi-Directional Fluid flow in Loudspeaker Ports," Preprint 6194, AES Convention 117 (2004); co-author: Zachary Rapoport

Howard Durbin:

"Three Dimensional Diaphragm Suspensions for Compression Drivers," JAES volume 28, number 10, pp. 720 - 725 (October 1980); co-author F. Murray

John Eargle:

Sound System Design Reference Manual, (Incorporating *Augspurger: Sound Workshop Manual*), 1982, 1986, 1999, JBL Professional

Handbook of Sound System Design, ELAR Publishing (Commack, NY, 1989)

Electroacoustical Reference Data, Van Nostrand Reinhold (New York 1990; reprinted by Kluwer Academic Publishers 2002)

Audio Engineering for Sound Reinforcement, JBL/Hal Leonard Corp. 2002; co-author Chris Foreman

Loudspeaker Handbook, Chapman & Hall (New York 1997 1/e, Kluwer Academic Publishers 2003 2/e)

"Loudspeakers," JAES volume 10, number 11, Oct/Nov 1977

"State of the Art Cinema Sound Reproduction Systems: Technical Advances and System Considerations," co-author: Mark Engebretson; Preprint 1799, AES Convention 69 (1981)

"Cinema Sound Reproduction Systems: Technical Advances and System Design Considerations," JSMPTE 91/11, Nov 1982; co-author M. Engebretson

"Improvements in Monitor Loudspeaker Systems," JAES volume 31, number 6 (June 1983); co-authors D. Smith and D. Keele

"A Microcomputer Program for Central Loudspeaker Array Design" (1983) co-authors: D. Albertz, D. B. Keele, R. Means Preprint 2028, AES Convention 74 (1983)

" Microcomputer Program for Determining Loudspeaker Coverage in Motion-Picture Theaters," JSMPTE volume 93, number 8 (August 1984); co-author: R. Means

"The Academy's New State-of-the-Art Loudspeaker System," JSMPTE volume 94, number 6 (June 1985); co-authors: J. Bonner and D. Ross

"An analysis of some Off-Axis Stereo Localization Problems," Preprint 2390, AES Convention 81 (1986); co-author: Greg Timbers

"A Summary of JBL's CADP (Central Array Design Program)," Presented at AES 6th International Conference on Sound Reinforcement, 5 - 8 May 1988, Paper 4B; co-author: S. Romeo

"Measurement and Estimation of Large Loudspeaker Array Performance," JAES volume 38, number 4 (April 1990); co-author: M. Gander. Also Preprint 2839, AES Convention 87 (1989)

"Digital System Integration in the Studio Monitoring Environment," Preprint 4036, AES 5th Australian Regional Convention (1995); co-authors: M. Gander and J. Eargle

"Direct Radiators Versus Horn Loading: Design Principles and Historical Perspectives in Sound Reinforcement" (1996) Proceedings of the Institute of Acoustics (UK) Volume 18: Part 8 (Reproduced Sound) co-author: Mark Gander

"Performance of Horn Systems: Low-Frequency Cut-off, Pattern Control, and Distortion Trade-Offs," Preprint 4330, AES Convention 101 (1996); co-author: W. Gelow

"Improvements in Motion Picture Sound: The Academy's New Three-Way Loudspeaker System," JSMPTE volume 106, number 7 (July 1997); co-authors D. Gray and M. Mayfield

"Cinema Sound Reproduction systems: Evolving Technical Requirements and Architectural Considerations." Preprint 4831, AES Convention 105 (1998); co-author: W. Gelow

"Historical Perspectives and Technology Overview of Loudspeakers for Sound Reinforcement," *JAES 52/4*, Apr 2004; co-author M. Gander

"Audio Monitoring in Contemporary Post-Production Environments," *JSMPTE* 114/1, Jan 2005

Mark Gander:

"Loudspeakers for Studio Monitoring and Musical Instruments," Chapter in J. Borwick: *Loudspeaker and Headphone Handbook-3rd edition*, Focal Press (London 2001)

Editor, *Loudspeakers Vol. 3: Systems and Crossover Networks*, AES Anthology, 1996

Editor, *Loudspeakers Vol. 4: Transducers, Measurement and Evaluation*, AES Anthology, 1996

"Theory and Practice in Audio Education: Experience of a Recent Graduate," JAES volume 26, number 11 (Nov 1978); first published in "Trends in Audio Education – A Symposium," Preprint 1379, AES Convention 60 (1978); in participation with others

"Moving-Coil Loudspeaker Topology as an Indicator of Linear Excursion Capability," JAES volume 29, number 1/2 (January/February 1981) Also Preprint 1554, AES Convention 64 (1979)

"Ground Plane Acoustic Measurements of Loudspeaker Systems," JAES volume 30, number 10 (October 1982) Also Preprint 1648, AES Convention 66 (1980)

"Dynamic Linearity and Power Compression in Moving-Coil Loudspeakers," JAES volume 34, number 9 pp. 627 - 646 (September 1986) Also Preprint 2128, AES Convention 76 (1984)

"Measurement and Estimation of Large Loudspeaker Array Performance," JAES volume 38, number 4, pp. 204 - 220 (April 1990); co-author J. Eargle. Also Preprint 2839, AES Convention 87 (1989)

"Digital System Integration in the Studio Monitoring Environment," Preprint 4036, AES 5th Australian Regional Convention (1995); co-authors: W. Gelow and J. Eargle

"Direct Radiators Versus Horn Loading: Design Principles and Historical Perspectives in Sound Reinforcement" (1996) Proceedings of the Institute of Acoustics (UK) Volume 18: Part 8 (Reproduced Sound); co-author: J. Eargle

"The Dual-Coil Drive Loudspeaker," Paper MAL-14, AES UK Conference on Microphones and Loudspeakers: The Ins and Outs of Audio (MAL, February 1998); co-author Douglas Button

"Historical Perspectives and Technology Overview of Loudspeakers for Sound Reinforcement," JAES volume 52, number 4 (Apr 2004); co-author J. Eargle

William J. Gelow:

"An Integrated Digital Concept in Studio Monitoring, "Engineering Symposium Record, EBU, 2nd Radio Montreux International Radio Symposium and Technical Exhibition (June 1994); co-authors M. Gander and J. Eargle

"Digital System Integration in the Studio Monitoring Environment," Preprint 4036, 5th Australian Regional AES convention (April 1995); co-authors M. Gander and J. Eargle

"Performance of Horn Systems: Low Frequency Cut-off, Pattern Control, and Distortion Trade-offs," Preprint 4330, AES Convention 101 (1996); co-author J. Eargle

"Cinema Sound Reproduction Systems: Evolving Technical Requirements and Architectural considerations, Preprint 4831, AES Convention 106 (1998); co-author J. Eargle

D. B. Keele:

"An Efficiency Constant Comparison Between Low-Frequency Horns and Direct Radiators," Preprint 1127, AES Convention 54 (1976)

"Low-Frequency Horn Design Using Thiele/Small Driver Parameters," Preprint 1250, AES Convention 57 (1977)

"AWASP: An Acoustic Wave Analysis and Simulation Program," Preprint 1365, AES Convention 60 (October 1978)

"Automated Loudspeaker Polar Response Measurements under Microcomputer Control," Preprint 1586, AES Convention 65 (October 1980)

"Direct Low-Frequency Driver Synthesis from System Specifications," JAES volume 30, number 11, pp. 800 - 814 (November 1982) Also Preprint 1797, AES Convention 69 (1981)

"A Microcomputer Program for Central Loudspeaker Array Design," Preprint 2028, AES Convention 74 (1983); co-authors: D. Albertz, J. Eargle, and R. Means

"Improvements in Monitor Loudspeaker Systems," JAES volume 31, number 6, pp. 408 - 422 (June 1983) Also Preprint 1784, AES Convention 69 (1981) co-authors: D. Smith and J. Eargle

"A Loudspeaker Horn that Covers a Flat Rectangular Area from an Oblique Angle," Preprint 2052, AES Convention 74 (1983)

"Effective Performance of Bessel Arrays," JAES volume 38, number 10, pp. 723-748 (October 1990) Also Preprint 2846, AES Convention 87 (1989)

"Maximum Efficiency of Direct-Radiator Loudspeakers," Preprint 3193, AES Convention 91 (1991)

"The Analytic Impulse and the Energy-Time Curve: The Debate Continues," Preprint 3399, Convention 93 (October 1992)

"Anechoic Chamber Walls: Should They be Resistive or Reactive at Low Frequencies?" JAES volume 42, number 6, pp. 454 - 466 (June 1994) Also Preprint 3572, AES Convention 94 (1993)

"The Application of Broadband Constant Beamwidth Transducer (CBT) Theory to Loudspeaker Arrays," Preprint 5216, AES Convention 99 (1995)

"Suspension Bounce as a Distortion Mechanism in Loudspeakers with a Progressive Stiffness," Preprint 5519, AES Convention 112 (2002)

"Implementation of Straight-Line and Flat-panel Constant Beamwidth Transducer (CBT) Loudspeaker Arrays using Signal Delays," Preprint 5653, AES Convention 113 (2002); co-author: R. Mikelich

"The Full-Sphere Sound Field of Constant Beamwidth Transducer (CBT) Loudspeaker Line Arrays," Preprint 5746, AES Convention 114 (2003)

"Comparison of Direct Radiator Loudspeaker
System nominal Power Efficiency vs. True
Efficiency with High-Bl drivers," Preprint
5887, AES Convention 115 (2003)

"Practical Implementation of Constant
Beamwidth Transducer (CBT) Loudspeaker
Circular Arc Line Arrays," Preprint
5863, AES Convention 115 (2003)

"Maximum Efficiency of Compression Drivers,"
Preprint 6193, AES Convention 117 (2004)

"Ground Plane Constant Beam Width
Transducer (CBT) Loudspeaker Circular-
Arc Arrays," Preprint 6594, AES Convention
119 (2005); co-author: D. Button

James B. Lansing:

"The Duplex Speaker," *Communications*
(December 1943)

"The Duplex Loudspeaker," Journal
SMPE, volume 43, number 3, pp,
168-173 (September 1944)

"An Improved Loudspeaker System for Theaters,"
Journal SMPE, volume 45, number 5, pp. 339-
349 (November 1945); co-author: John Hilliard

Bart Locanthi:

"Theater Loudspeaker system Incorporating
an Acoustic Lens Radiator," JSMPTE,
volume 63, number 9 (September
1954); co-author: John Frayne

"An Ultra-Low Distortion Direct-Current
Amplifier," JAES volume 15, number
3, pp. 290 - 294 (July 1967)

"Application of Electronic Circuit Analogies
to Loudspeaker Design Problems."
JAES volume 19, number 9, pp. 778 - 785
(October 1971); reprinted from IRE Transactions
on Audio, volume PGA-6, March 1952

Edmund May:

"Five-Inch High Efficiency Wide Range
Loudspeaker for Small Enclosures,"
Preprint 499, AES Convention 31 (1966)

Fancher Murray:

"The Motional Impedance of a Electro-
Dynamic Loudspeaker," presented at the
98th Meeting of the Acoustical Society of
America, 19 November 1979; Paper T12

"Three Dimensional Diaphragm Suspensions
for Compression Drivers," JAES volume
28, number 10, pp. 720 - 725 (October
1980) co-author H. Durbin

"Measurement of Transducer Motional Impedance –
An Update." Preprint 2510, AES Convention
83 (October 1987) co-author. D. Siefert

"MTF as a Tool in Transducer Selection,"
presented at the AES 6th Internal Conference
on Sound Reinforcement, 5 May 1988, Paper 9F

"The Voice Coil and Eddy Currents," Preprint
3902, AES Convention 97 (October 1994)

Garry Margolis:

"Personal Calculator Program for Low Frequency Horn Design Using Thiele-Small Driver Parameters," Preprint 1433, AES Convention 62 (October 1979); co-author J. Young

"Personal Calculator Programs for Approximate Vented-Box and Closed-Box Loudspeaker System Design," JAES volume 29, number 6, pp. 421 - 440; co-author R. Small; also Preprint 1650, AES Convention 66 (1980)

Sean Olive:

"Hearing is Believing vs. Believing is Hearing: Blind vs. Sighted Listening Tests and Other Interesting Things," Preprint 3894, AES Convention 97 (1994); co-author: F. Toole

"A Method for Training of Listeners and Selecting Program Material for Listening Tests," Preprint 3893, AES Convention 97 (1994)

"Separating Fact from Fiction Through Listening Tests," Proceedings of the 1995 DSPx Technical Program, pp. 454 - 463 (1995)

"The Variability of Loudspeaker Sound Quality Among Four Domestic-Sized Rooms." Preprint 4092, AES Convention 99 (1995); co-authors: P. Schuck, J. Ryan, S. Sally, M. Bonneville

"The Detection Thresholds of Resonances at Low Frequencies," JAES volume 45, number 3, pp. 116 - 128 (March 1997); co-authors: P. Schuck, J. Ryan, S. Sally, M. Bonneville

"A New Laboratory for Evaluating Multichannel Systems and Audio Components," Preprint 4842, AES Convention 105 (1998); co-authors: F. Toole and B. Castro

"Subjective Evaluation," Chapter in J. Borwick, *Loudspeaker and Headphone Handbook, 3rd edition*, Focal Press (London 2001); co-author: F. Toole

"Difference in Performance and Preference of Trained Vs. Untrained Listeners in Loudspeaker Tests: A Cast Study," JAES, volume 51, number 9, pp. 806 - 825 (October 2003)

"Multiple Regression Model for Predicting Loudspeaker Preference Using Objective Measurements, Parts 1 and 2," Preprints 6113 and 6190, AES Conventions 116 (2004) and 117 (2004)

Alex Salvatti:

"Maximizing Performance from Loudspeaker Ports," JAES volume 50, number 1 (December 2001); co-author D. Button; also Preprint 4855, AES Convention 105 (1998)

David Scheirman:

"Practical Considerations for Fiield Deployment of Modular Line Array Systems," AES Conference number 21, St Petersburg, Russia (2002)

Gregory Timbers:

"New Lows in Home-Built Subwoofers," *Audio Magazine*, August 1983; co-author: Lorr Kramer

"An analysis of some Off-Axis Stereo Localization Problems" (1986) co-author: J. Eargle; Preprint 2390 (Convention 81)

Floyd Toole:

"Subjective Evaluation," Chapter 11 in J. Borwick, *Loudspeaker and Headphone Handbook*, Focal Press (London, 1994)

"Subjective Evaluation," Chapter in J. Borwick, *Loudspeaker and Headphone Handbook, 3rd edition*, Focal Press (London 2001); co-author: S. Olive

"Sound Reproducing Systems," *McGraw-Hill Encyclopedia of Science and Technology*, 9th edition, McGraw-Hill (New York)

"Hearing is Believing vs. Believing is Hearing: Blind vs. Sighted Listening Tests and Other Interesting Things," Preprint 3894, AES Convention 97 (1994); co-author: S. Olive

"A New Laboratory for Evaluating Multichannel Systems and Audio Components," Preprint 4842, AES Convention 105 (1998); co-authors: S. Olive and B. Castro

"The Acoustics and Psychoacoustics of Loudspeakers and Rooms – The Stereo Past and the Multichannel Future," Preprint 5201, AES Convention 109 (2000)

"Loudspeakers and Rooms for Sound Reproduction – a Scientific Review," JAES volume 54, number 6, pp. 451 - 476 (June 2006)

Mark Ureda:

"On the Movement of a Horn's Acoustic Center," Preprint 4986, AES Convention 106 (1999)

"Line Arrays: Theory and Applications." Preprint 5304, AES Convention 110 (2001)

"J" and "Spiral" Line Arrays," Preprint 5485, AES Convention 111 (2001)

"Pressure Response of Line Sources," Preprint 5649, AES Convention 113 (2002)

"Analysis of Loudspeaker Line Arrays," JAES volume 52, number 5, pp. 467 - 495 (May 2004)

Todd Welti:

"How Many Subwoofers are Enough?" Preprint 5602, AES Convention 112 (2002)

"Subjective comparison of Single Channel vs. Two Channel subwoofer Reproduction," Preprint 6332, AES Convention 117 (2002)

"In-Room Low Frequency Optimization," Preprint 5942, AES Convention 115 (2003); co-author: A. Devantier

Section 2: Patents Granted to JBL Engineering Staff.

A sampling of both utility patents covering fundamental principles as well as design patents covering form and appearance are listed. Only U. S. Patents are listed; in many cases international patents have also been applied for and granted.

Utility Patents: 2,815,086: Convertible Loudspeaker system; JBL Hartsfield. Granted 3 December 1957 to William L. Hartsfield.

3,065,816: Stereophonic sound distributor; JBL Paragon, Metregon, and Minigon. Granted 27 November 1962 to Richard H. Ranger.

4,039,243: Electrical connector; speaker twist-locking input terminals, Granted 2 August 1977 to Paul D. Johnson.

4,308,932: Loudspeaker horn; basic Bi-Radial® horn design. Granted 5 January to D. B. Keele.

4,324,312: Diaphragm suspension construction; diamond surround pattern used in JBL compression drivers and tweeters. Granted 13 April 1982 to Howard Durbin.

4,508,655: Defined coverage loudspeaker horn; basic asymmetrical Bi-Radial® design. Granted 8 April 1986 to D. B. Keele.

4,655,316: Acoustic diaphragm; ribbed titanium dome, used in JBL compression drivers and tweeters. Granted 7 April 1987 to Fancher Murray.

5,042,072: Phasing plug for compression driver. Granted 26 May 1992 to David Bie.

5,143,339: Speaker mounting assembly; spring-loading of transducer in a box. Granted 1 September 1992 to Dan Ashcraft and Steve Romeo.

5,438,625: Arrangement to correct the linear and nonlinear transfer behavior of electro-acoustical transducers. Granted 1 August 1995 to Wolfgang Klippel.

5,533,132: Loudspeaker thermal management structure; basis of EON® thermal system. Granted 2 July 1996 to Douglas Button.

5,602,366: Spaceframe with array positioning element; used in HLA products. Granted 11 February 1997 to William Gelow and Mick Whelan.

5,664,023: Low TCR wire in high power audio coils. Granted 2 September 1997 to Douglas Button.

5,704,578: Front-loading swivel ball loudspeaker mount; basis of Invisiball® mounting scheme. Granted 6 January 1998 to Roy Fischer.

5,748,760: Dual coil drive with multipurpose housing; basic Differential Drive® patent for transducers. Granted 5 May 1998 to Douglas Button.

5,828,767: Inductive braking in a dual coil speaker driver unit; refinement of Differential Drive®; used in LSR6300 Series studio monitors. Granted 27 July 1998 to Douglas Button.

6,466,680: High frequency loudspeaker module for cinema screen; covers screen spreading compensation in ScreenArray® products. Granted 15 October 2002 to Bernard Werner and William Gelow.

6,513,622: Full range loudspeaker system for cinema screen; covers ScreenArray® products. Granted 4 February 2003 to Bernard Werner and William Gelow.

6,768,806: Shorting rings in dual-coil dual-gap loudspeaker drivers for distortion reduction. Granted 27 July 2004 to Douglas Button, Alex Salvatti, and Ralph Hyde.

6,774,510: Electromagnetic motor with flux stabilization ring, saturation tips, and radiator; used in ferrite dual coil drivers. Granted 10 August 2004 to Douglas Button and Jerry Moro.

6,801,634: Loudspeaker coil suspension system; coil pocket assembly used in 2430-Series drivers. Granted 5 October 2004 to Douglas Button and Alex Salvatti.

6,847,726: Shorting rings in dual-coil dual-gap loudspeaker drivers; for distortion reduction in Differential Drive® transducers. Granted 25 January 2005 to Douglas Button, Alex Salvatti, and Ralph Hyde.

6,952,874: Two-stage phasing plug system in a compression driver; used in 2430-series drivers. Granted 11 October 2005 to Douglas Button and Alex Salvatti.

7,072,481: Additional features of two-stage phasing plug system in a compression driver. Granted 4 July 2006 to Douglas Button and Alex Salvatti.

7,027,605: Mid-range loudspeaker. Granted 11 April 2006 to Bernard Werner.

7,095,869: Loudspeaker coil suspension system; additional features of coil pocket assembly; used in 2430-series compression drivers. Granted 22 August 2006 to Douglas J. Button.

Design Patents: D247,490: Loudspeaker assembly, for Aquarius products. Granted 14 March 1978 to Patrick Everidge.

D266,420: Loudspeaker magnet housing; ferrite magnet tire for SFG transducers. Granted 5 October 1982 to Douglas Warner.

D267,644: Loudspeaker magnet housing; ferrite magnet tire for SFG magnet, LE8 and LE10 type transducers. Granted 5 October 1982 to Douglas Warner

D379,629: Loudspeaker enclosure; for large EON enclosure. Granted 3 June 1997 to Richard Watson and Ronald Vish.

D393,860: Loudspeaker enclosure; for small EON enclosure. Granted 28 April 1998 to Richard Watson.

D394,263: Loudspeaker enclosure; for Contractor Control® Series. Granted 12 May 1998 to Roy Fischer.

D439,237: Loudspeaker enclosure: for SRX products. Granted 20 March 2001 to Victor Felix.

D450,683: Integrated baffle design for a loudspeaker; for MPro products. Granted 20 November 2001 to Mary Vosse.

D450,778: Radiation boundary integrator for a loudspeaker system; RBI for VerTec® products. Granted 20 November 2001 to Mark Engebretson.

D452,964: Acoustical horn; for MPro product. Granted 15 January 2002 to Mary Vosse.

D483,743: Speaker transducer housing; used in 2260-Series transducers. Granted 16 December 2003 to Mary Vosse.

D483,744: Portion of a speaker transducer housing; for 8-inch Differential Drive transducer. Granted 16 December 2003 to Mary Vosse.

Selected Patent Illustrations:

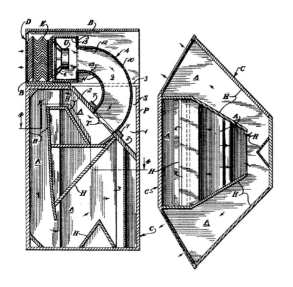

Figure 14-1. U. S. Patent 2,815,086
"JBL Hartsfield"

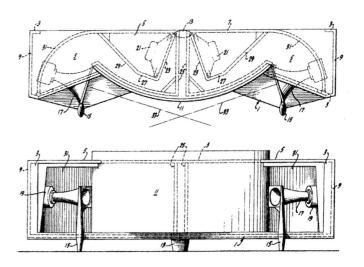

Figure 14-2. U. S. Patent 3,065,816
"JBL Paragon"

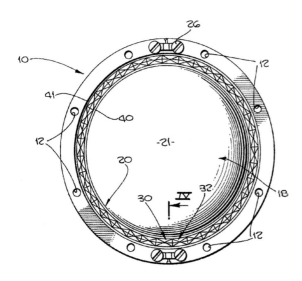

Figure 14-3. U. S. Patent 4,324,312
"Diamond Surround"

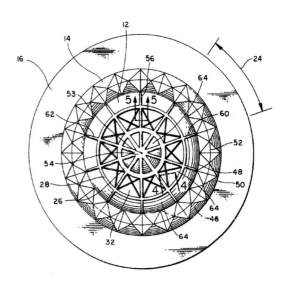

Figure 14-4. U. S. Patent 4,655,316
"Ribbed Titanium Diaphragm"

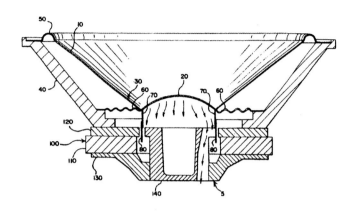

Figure 14-5. U. S. Patent 5,042,072
"Vented Gap Cooling"

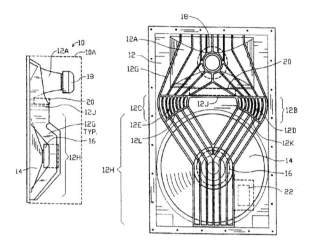

Figure 14-6. U. S. Patent 5,533,132
"EON Thermal Management"

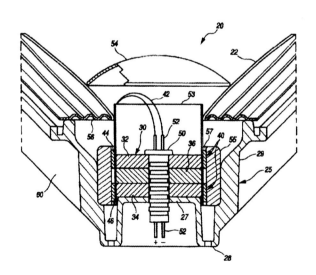

Figure 14-7. U. S. Patent 5,748,760
"Differential Drive"

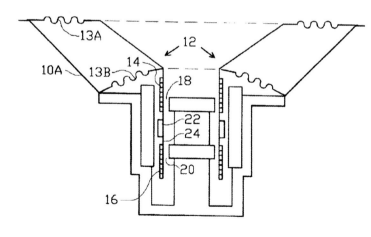

Figure 14-8. U. S. Patent
5,828,767 "Inductive Braking"

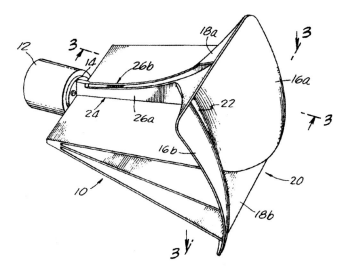

Figure 14-9. U. S. Patent 4,308,932
"Basic Bi-Radial Horn Design"

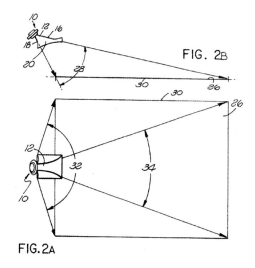

Figure 14-10. U. S. Patent 4,580,655 "Basic
Defined Coverage Horn Design"

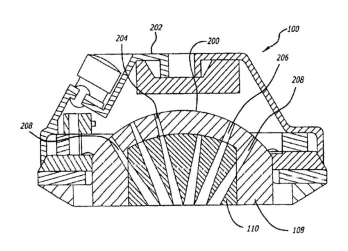

Figure 14-11. U. S. Patent 7,072,481
"Two-stage Phasing Plug System
in a Compression Driver"

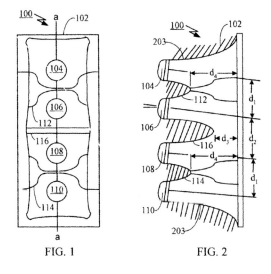

Figure 14-12. U. S. Patent 7,027,605
"Mid-range Loudspeaker"

Index